# PRAISE FOR MIKE SAGER

"Like his journalistic precursors Tom Wolfe and Hunter S. Thompson, Sager writes frenetic, off-kilter pop-sociological profiles of Americans in all their vulgarity and vitality...He writes with flair, but only in the service of an omnivorous curiosity and defies expectations in pieces that lesser writers would play for satire or sensationalism... A Whitmanesque ode to teeming humanity's mystical unity."
—*New York Times Book Review*

"Mike Sager writes about places and events we seldom get a look at—and people from whom we avert our eyes. But with Sager in command of all the telling details, he shows us history, humanity, humor, sometimes even honor. He makes us glad to live with our eyes wide open."
—Richard Ben Cramer, Pulitzer Prize-winning author of *What It Takes: The Way to the White House*

"Like a silver-tongued Margaret Mead, Sager slips into foreign societies almost unnoticed and lives among the natives, chronicling his observations in riveting long-form narratives."
—*Performances*

"Mike Sager is the Beat poet of American journalism, that rare reporter who can make literature out of shabby reality. Equal parts reporter, ethnographer, stylist and cultural critic, Sager has for 40 years carried the tradition of Tom Wolfe on his broad shoulders, chronicling the American scene and psyche. Nobody does it sharper, smarter, or with more style."
—Walt Harrington, author of *Acts of Creation*

## ALSO BY MIKE SAGER

*The Lonely Hedonist*

*Stoned Again*

*The Devil and John Holmes*

*High Tolerance, A Novel*

*The Someone You're Not*

*Revenge of the Donut Boys*

*Scary Monsters and Super Freaks*

*Vetville*

*Hunting Marlon Brando*

# JANET'S WORLD

## THE INSIDE STORY OF THE WASHINGTON POST PULITZER FABULIST

### MIKE SAGER

JANET'S WORLD: The Inside Story of
Washington Post Pulitzer Fabulist Janet Cooke

Copyright © 2003, 2013 by Mike Sager

All rights reserved. No part of this publication may be reproduced, stored in a retrieval system, or transmitted, in any form or by any means, electronic, mechanical, photocopying, recording, or otherwise, without the prior written permission of the publisher. Published in the United States of America.

Cataloging-in-Publication data for this book is available from the Library of Congress.
ISBN 13:
Paperback: 978-1-950154-17-3
eBook: 978-0-9881785-8-8

Cover Design and Illustration by WBYK.com.au
Interior design by Siori Kitajima, SF AppWorks LLC
(SFAppworks.com)

Published by The Sager Group LLC
TheSagerGroup.net
In Cooperation with NeoText (NeoTextCorp.com)

# JANET'S WORLD

## THE INSIDE STORY OF THE WASHINGTON POST PULITZER FABULIST

## MIKE SAGER

April 15, 1981

"Jimmy's World" was in essence a fabrication. I never encountered or interviewed an 8-year-old heroin addict. The September 28, 1981, article in The Washington Post was a serious misrepresentation which I deeply regret. I apologize to my newspaper, my profession, the Pulitzer board and all seekers of the truth. Today, in facing up to the truth, I have submitted my resignation.

*Janet Cooke*

*Janet Cooke touched off the biggest scandal in the history of modern journalism when her Pulitzer Prize-winning article, about an eight-year-old heroin addict, published by the Washington Post, turned out to be a fraud. Cooke's only in-depth telling of her own story.*

She sashayed into the acre-square newsroom of the *Washington Post* on the third day of 1980, wearing a red wool suit over a white silk shirt, the neck opened casually to the second button, exposing a thin gold chain, a teasing glimpse of lingerie, the slight swell of a milk-chocolate breast. Her long acrylic nails gleaming in the hard fluorescent light, she made her way down a long aisle between the desk pods of the Metro section toward the Weekly section, carrying her cashmere coat, oversized purse and soft leather briefcase—inside of which she carried, like a girl on her first day of school, pads, pens, maps, two pairs of glasses, a spare pair of black tights, and a pink knit sweater for the back of her chair.

As she passed, heads turned, eyes bugged, people whispered and winked and smirked. They swiveled around in their chairs and tracked the pleasing sway of her hips, the jaunty bounce of her long, Marie Antoinette ringlets, a mass of dark, lacquered curls trailing past her shoulder blades. Men and women, editors and reporters, distinguished members of the press, they clucked their tongues over the shortness of her pleated skirt, the self-possessed coolness of her gait. For years the customary greeting in the newsroom had been "What's the gossip?" At the moment, this clearly was it.

Her name was Janet Cooke. Six months earlier, when her letter and CV had crossed *Post* executive editor Ben Bradlee's desk—on one of those slow afternoons when he would occupy himself by reading unsolicited applications from reporters around the world—the brass-balled legend had sat up abruptly in his chair. Before him, as he might have said, was a fuckin' wet dream: twenty-five years old, Phi Beta Kappa from Vassar, master's in literature, fluent in two foreign languages, television experience, one writing award in two years at the *Toledo Blade*, member of the National Association of Black Journalists.

As the newsroom had yet to convert to computer, Bradlee took up a red grease pencil and circled "Phi Beta Kappa," "Vassar" and "Black Journalists." At a time when papers were just beginning their perilous journey toward "newsroom diversity," here was the ideal candidate—an Ivy League twofer with a résumé of gold. He sent Janet's letter along to Metro editor Bob Woodward, noting that she should be recruited before The New York Times or the networks scooped her up.

After her two, day-long interviews in D.C., with *Post* brass and ranking members of the paper's informal Black caucus, and *even* with Watergate investigator Woodward—who was being given a chance, as the assistant managing editor in charge of the Metro section, to try his hand at management, with an eye perhaps to Bradlee's chair. It was Woodward himself who'd called Janet and offered her the job. Later he would joke how tough she'd been, negotiating for a later start date and five thousand more in salary.

Now it was her first day, and she was almost two hours late, having lost her way walking the three blocks from her hotel to work. Over the coming weeks and months, the layout of L'Enfant's capital city would elude Janet dramatically. Driving four blocks to a grocery store, she'd end up miles away in Maryland. The two-mile commute to work from her apartment in fashionable Adams Morgan—from her parking place at her apartment to her parking place near the *Post*, the route required two left turns and a right—routinely took an hour. On assignment she'd struggle through the streets in her sporty green Datsun 240Z. She'd pull over, cry a little, consult her map, set out again. Finally, magically, she'd arrive at the place she'd been searching for, and her work could commence.

As she strolled so erect and proud and seemingly in control down the long aisle toward the Weekly, she had no idea she was causing such a stir. In fact, so constant was the turmoil of self-doubt inside her head that she rarely knew what was happening around her. From the earliest age Janet's father had instilled one desperate and overriding philosophy that haunted her every step: *Because you're a girl, because you're black, you must do everything twice as well as anybody else. There is no room for screwing up. There is no slack. Even if you're better you will never be considered the best.*

Had she been able, Janet would have noticed her entrance into the newsroom was garnering her just the kind of reaction she had always worked for and wished for and dreamed about. Since she was young, wherever she went, people had taken notice. They'd measure her accomplishments, her stunning looks, her regal aspect. In high school kids called her the Ice Princess, so cool and intimidating did she seem. Of course, the read was 180 degrees off. In Janet's own mind, she was more of a "frog." She had secrets, horrible secrets, that nobody knew. Walking down the aisle toward her future at the *Post*, she remembers feeling "like Jell-O, just very shaky, really frightened, and totally unsure." *What if I'm not good enough?* she agonized.

Nevertheless, Janet carried on as she always did, plying the industrial carpet in her sensible black pumps, holding her chin high, hooding her large almond eyes, aiming them straight ahead. Trying to calm herself, she concentrated on some of her mother's maxims, little recipes for living that had stuck with her though the years. *Be cleaner than clean, more polite than polite. Pay too much attention to others and they're likely to pay too much attention to you.* As was her practice in pressure situations, Janet sang to herself, an old favorite song from the musical *The King* and I, "I Whistle a Happy Tune." *Whenever I feel afraid, I hold my head erect, and whistle a happy tune, and no one ever knows I'm afraid.*

"That's my anthem," she would joke, eyelids fluttering, full lips curling upward into a mischievous grin. And then she'd laugh—a low-pitched giggle, sultry and suggestive and rather devil-may-care; her trademark, her smoke screen.

After what felt like an endless walk down the aisle, Janet arrived at the Weekly section, next to the glass offices occupied by Woodward and columnist Richard Cohen. She was met by Stan Hinden, editor of the three zoned local editions that comprised the Weekly section, one of the nation's earlier experiments with zoned local editions. Launched in reaction to the recent boom of "neighbor papers" across the nation, the Weeklies were tasked with touching the home lives of subscribers, bringing the world-famous institution back to its roots as a local daily. Designed to be a "paper within the paper," the section featured happy four-color fronts, good-news stories, calendars of events, roadwork listings, and a commuter columnist called Dr. Gridlock.

The Weeklies were considered a kind of in-house farm team—some said boot camp—staffed with summer interns, two-year interns, and a number of probationers and misfits who'd had trouble in other sections or were nearing retirement age. In short, nobody who worked on the Weekly fit the mold of the idealized *Washington Post* reporter, Bradlee himself—a dashing, brilliant, connected, roguish ivy league liberal who was known for his friendship with John F. Kennedy and his marriage to celebrity journalist Sally Quinn. Almost from the beginning, Janet noticed the difference between the Weekly and the rest of the paper. In time, she'd begin referring to her assignment as "the ghetto," and "the back of the bus." She'd joke that her parents had spent lots of money sending her to private schools in order to keep her out of such circumstances. Internally she'd wonder: If she was good enough to be hired by the *Post*, why wasn't she good enough to be part of the "real" staff? *What is wrong with me?*

At last she was greeted by Stan Hinden, a kindly, white-haired, Jewish grandfather who stood five-foot-two. Where most in the newsroom were called by their last names, he was universally known as Stan. Janet was five-foot-eight. Her new boss reached up and relieved her of her coat, then led her to the closet, showed her which hook she could use. Then he led Janet to the desk of her new editor, Vivian Aplin-Brownlee. A light-skinned black woman from Texas, Aplin-Brownlee was known for her prickly tongue, her skill in office politics, and her fine touch as an editor. Many likened her to a drill sergeant, someone who fondly, ruthlessly tore you down in order to build you back up—Lou Gossett with a short Afro, dangling earrings and oversized glasses.

Like most of the black staffers at the time, Vivian was equally fluent in the King's English and the language of the streets, the first used with whites, the second only with hipsters and other blacks. At the time, Washington was nearly seventy percent black; the residents openly, gleefully, called it Chocolate City. Janet had never encountered such a place; neither had she met black people like those in Washington. Always the lone black girl in the crowd of white faces, Janet did not speak jive.

During her first job interview at the *Post*, Janet met Dorothy Gilliam, the grande dame of black female columnists. Gilliam asked what Janet thought the role of a black reporter should be. Janet was shocked by the question. She had never dated a black man. She had never had a black girlfriend. On the bus home from school one day during her sophomore year, two of the black boys from her high school doused her with baby powder so she would look the color she acted. Janet didn't know black people, never got along with them. She'd been raised to believe, however conflictedly, that race didn't matter, that it was not a crucial factor in determining an individual's life. In many ways, Janet thought like a white person: She was frequently accused by other blacks of being an Oreo, meaning black on the outside, white on the inside. It was not very far from the truth. As a child, before bed each night, she would pray on her knees: "Please, God, let me wake up blonde."

To Gilliam's question, Janet responded that the first thing a black reporter should do is not think of herself as any color. She should just go out, find the story, come back, and write it.

Gilliam looked stunned. "Why, you poor silly little girl," she exclaimed.

Thankfully, Janet's meeting with Gilliam had not counted against her. She was hired and she was here, standing in the Weekly on her first day of work. After meeting Hinden and Aplin-Brownlee and being introduced to a number of other new co-workers, Janet felt so welcomed that her anxiety eased a bit, she was able to take in her surroundings. She was impressed with the vastness of the room, a full acre that stretched over three interconnected buildings. Everything was so bright; just like the movie *All the President's Men*, which had been shot in this very room with Robert Redford and Dustin Hoffman and all the rest. It also impressed her that so many of the people sitting at the desks around her looked so young. From where she was standing, she could see Bob Woodward speaking on the phone in his glass office. A guy who was going down in history was actually her boss. Hell, he'd hired her personally.

At some point there came a lull in the conversation—one of those uncomfortable silences where everybody's standing around in the middle of the office and nobody knows what to do next.

"So," Janet ventured, "where do I sit?"

Hinden's smile disappeared. He scratched his head and surveyed his fiefdom, looking this way and that.

Seconds ticked by.

Beneath her calm and beautiful exterior, Janet began to roil.

Hinden led a little tour, walking from desk to desk, trying to find a suitable space for his new prize. Janet followed two steps behind, mortified, the voice inside her head growing more sarcastic, more hysterical:

*Jesus Christ, this is the Washington fucking Post. Can't they find me a desk?*

"I just finally decided I want my life back," Janet Cooke says.

She is sitting on a public bench at the Crossroads shopping mall, near Kalamazoo, Michigan, sixteen years after her first day at the *Post*. The temperature outside hovers cruelly below zero; snow is piled high in the parking lot; the light is thin; the landscape is a featureless clutter of stoplights and franchises. Inside, there is the usual Muzak and kitsch of the modern mall-as-town-square, with mothers strolling babies, women talking in tones of confidence, retirees hoofing laps around the perimeter, "trying their best to outwalk death," as Janet says with characteristic wit.

Though she has gained a few pounds and now favors black clothes over dramatic reds and royal purples, and clunky Dr. Marten boots over sensible pumps, her hair is still long and luxurious, her nails highly polished, and her air—the outside presentation, at least—is still confident, intelligent, commanding and playfully sexual. Despite the years and the circumstances, Janet is known among her co-workers as Miss Cooke—or Miss Kitty to her very small circle of intimates. In a few minutes, she will sigh and head toward Hudson's department store for her $6 an hour shift at the Liz Claiborne boutique, selling midmarket women's wear.

On September 28, 1980, nine months and fifty-two bylines into her tenure at the *Post*, Janet caused a worldwide sensation with her front-page story, "Jimmy's World," about an eight-year-old heroin addict who lived in the nation's capital and aspired to nothing more in life than a future of selling and doing drugs. On April 13, 1981—after the Pulitzer committee, enthusiastic about both her writing and her status as a black female, juggled her entry from the local-news to the features category in order to assure her a prize—Janet was given a Pulitzer, the most coveted award in daily journalism. Two days later, after discrepancies in her resume were discovered, Janet confessed that "Jimmy's World" was actually a work of fiction. Disgraced, the *Post* returned the Pulitzer. Janet resigned.

Since then, Janet has become one of the most infamous figures in journalism. Google and other databases list thousands of entries under her name; her case has come to symbolize myriad transgressions, from plagiarism and fabrication to the use of unnamed sources, minority recruitment, newsroom ethics, résumé fraud, and even the precarious practice of New Journalism, where less skillful and principled writers have been known to take license in the pursuit of more literary work. Universally vilified from the moment her transgression was revealed, constantly dogged by the press (which never got a good crack at her in the days before paparazzi and tabloid TV characterized the mediascape), Janet has spent her life on the run—first as the wife of an American diplomat in Paris, more recently as a divorced, nearly destitute part-time retail clerk in Toledo, Ohio, Ann Arbor and Kalamazoo, Michigan. Later, she would begin anew in an undisclosed location and live a quiet and anonymous life under a different professional name.

Except for a short interview with Phil Donahue on the Today show about a year after her debacle, Janet never spoke out or gave voice to her version of the events that would forever change journalism. In late 1995, after some years of irregular correspondence—during which time I advised her as an editor, mentor, cheerleader and old friend about an autobiography she was hoping to write—Janet switched course. Fearing a first-person account would sound too self-serving, she asked me to write her story for *GQ*. Her objectives: a renewed writing career and, more important, the retrieval of her name from the files of infamy. "If Richard Nixon's name can be rehabilitated," she asks, "can't Janet Cooke's?" She is kidding, but not kidding at all.

This is Janet's exclusive story. Though I was picked as a sympathetic author, I will try my best to convey the incidents faithfully. The day Janet first sashayed into the *Post* newsroom, I was a twenty-three-year-old staff writer working under Woodward on the City staff of the Metro section. A former copy boy with only slight previous experience at an Atlanta alternative weekly, I found myself surrounded, during my six-year tenure in Metro, by a heady array of future media stars. There was future Pulitzer winner David Maraniss, future bestselling author and sports commentator John Feinstein, future TV reporter Michel McQueen. Michael Isikoff would go on to break the Bill Clinton/Monica Lewinsky affair. Neil Henry would become interim dean of the journalism school at Berkeley. Fellow writers included Chris Dickey, the son of former U.S. Poet Laureate James, and Ted Gup, Chip Brown, Blaine Harden, Patrick Tyler, Art Harris, Pete Earley, Ben Weiser, Sara Rimer, Molly Moore, Stephanie Mansfield, and many others—I believe it was said at the time that the *Post* employed 900 reporters and editors; the elder statesmen of the *Post* at the time were well known; we in Metro's training ground were seen as "the kids."

By dint of hours and circumstance, I met Janet late one night in the newsroom soon after her arrival. By the end of February, we had begun a love affair. It ended officially in June, but hung on—a painful, exhilarating psychodrama—for another year.

Janet was beautiful. She is as smart as any woman I have ever known. She had a deft command of language, humor, irony and detail; she could trade barbs and insights and stories with the best. She was passionate; she was vulnerable and needy; she brought out the best and worst in a man. She liked to leave little thoughtful notes in odd places, to buy sweet little gifts. She could find, in a cobwebbed larder, the ingredients for a midnight snack. She made cookies with Godiva chocolate. She was formidable.

And, as much as it pains me to say, she was a liar. It was her lying that killed my love, my trust, our relationship. There were small white lies and large, ornate fabrications. In the years following our breakup, every now and then I would encounter a piece of information I had always thought was fact, only to remember that Janet had been the source.

After the Pulitzer was returned, I was suspected of collaborating on "Jimmy's World," my name having been found on the "edit trial" of the *Post's* computer system. Bob Woodward grilled me twice over two days. He is, I discovered, as good as they say. Had I something to confess, I surely would have.

Janet's mental state and her dependence on me, between August and April, was such that I found myself, just before the announcement of the Pulitzers, on a jet to Europe. I needed to get away. By then twenty-four, I was out of my league in a very grown-up game.

I read about Janet's award in the *International Herald Tribune* on a ferry between Dover and Calais. In the train station, I sent her a telegram: "Standing ovations." Two days later, walking down the Champs-Elysées, I saw the headline: REPORTER CONFESSES STORY SUBJECT FAKED. I became dizzy and disoriented. I crumbled to a seat on the curb, feet in the gutter, as cars and people whizzed by.

The day "Jimmy's World" had run, all those months before, I'd had burgers at the Post Pub with Pat Tyler and Joe Pichirallo, both respected investigative reporters on Metro, two of my buds on a staff that was extremely social and close.

I think, like a good journalist, I wanted to get my thoughts on the record. "Jimmy's World," I predicted, would win the Pulitzer. Then it would be revealed as a fake.

I followed up immediately by telling Tyler and Pichirallo that I had no factual evidence for this conclusion. I didn't know *how* I knew this. Indeed, I wasn't sure my feelings weren't just jealousy. Given the writer and the story, you could see big prizes coming from a mile away. But I also knew that the story didn't feel right. The dialogue as written, for instance, sounded like a white person imitating black speech. Blacks in D.C.'s ghettos didn't say, "I be goin'." They said, "I goin'." And the appointments in the shooting gallery she described visiting—matching chrome-and-glass tables? Could Janet, with her terrible sense of direction, even have found Jimmy's house at night?

I had no evidence, just instinct.

Because I was a friend, I never asked.

I didn't want to know.

Despite the reams of commentary and discussion that have accumulated in the interim, I have always felt that no one has ever understood this whole sorry mess, the Janet Cooke affair. For all the attempts to render Janet's transgressions into civic and journalistic lessons, her actions, from where I sat, had nothing to do with social, political or philosophical issues. They had nothing to do with newspaper ethics or the First Amendment. Writing "Jimmy's World" was a highly personal act in a highly personal drama, a choice of action best explained, perhaps, as a damaged person's attempt to right the wrongs of her past, to overcome the paralyzing condition of self-loathing and self-doubt.

The truth is, Janet wasn't trying to win a Pulitzer. She wasn't out for fame and glory. New to the business and to the big time, she had no idea how hard a story like "Jimmy's World" could hit. Janet never considered the ramifications of lying to Ben Bradlee, Bob Woodward, one million Post readers and millions more worldwide.

"A Pulitzer was not her endgame," said Vivian Aplin-Brownlee, who died in 2007 at age sixty-one. "She just wanted to get out of the *Weekly*, away from me."

Simply put: Janet needed a story to turn in.

She didn't have one.

She wrote it anyway.

"What I did was wrong," she admits, her head and eyes lowering. "I regret that I did it. I was guilty. I did it, and I'm sorry that I did it. I'm ashamed that I did it."

She also says this: "What I did was horrible; believe me, I think that. But I don't think that in this particular case the punishment has fit the crime. I've lost my voice. I've lost half of my life. The girl who once spent eight dollars on a bottle of designer olive oil is now in a situation where cereal has become a viable dinner choice. It is my fault that I've never spoken up. But that's part of growing. I was a twenty-seven-year-old kid then. I'm forty-plus now. And I'm starting to understand some things about life, about my life. If people only understood why this really happened, maybe they'd have a different take on things. Maybe they'd think I wasn't so evil."

Janet Leslie Cooke was born somewhat unexpectedly in the tenth year of a stormy, four-decade marriage between Loretta and Stratman Cooke.

Her father, the eldest of five boys from a poor family in Alabama, attended the Tuskegee Institute and served as one of the famous black Airmen. Loretta Cooke was born in Hillsborough, the eldest of nine children. She was in high school when Stratman came to town; though he was nearly five years older, she picked him out as a boy who was going places, who represented the promise of a comfortable, middle class existence, one just beginning to be open to black people, modeled after the white American dream. At the time, even a woman with a high school education had to strap herself to a man. A future on her own could never have been considered, just as later, when her marriage became a nightmare, a future as a divorced mother with two girls could never have been considered. The pair eloped, then settled in Toledo, where Stratman finished his engineering degree. She worked in a local ordnance plant, a Rosie the Riveter type at the close of World War II.

Upon graduation Stratman found a job as an air-conditioning repairman for Toledo Edison. Cooke family lore recalls Stratman encountering the company's president one day in the halls of the headquarters. They spoke; the big man was impressed. "You got a suit, boy?" he asked Stratman.

In the ensuing years, Stratman studied law and opened a private practice, meanwhile continuing his rise at Toledo Edison. He retired as corporate secretary. He refused to be interviewed for this story. He has since died. Loretta Cooke also declined. For the last fifteen years, she has been the only press contact for Janet. Now that Janet's finally ready, says Loretta Cooke, she can speak for herself.

Her father, Janet remembers, "was very smart, very handsome, very mean, very rigid." Though he made fun for years, Janet says, of "negroes and their love affair with Cadillacs," he drove a Cadillac for more than three decades, updating every couple of years. Until his death, he lived in the house where Janet was raised, a big, old converted duplex right at the edge of the inner city, in a black district that is neither ghetto nor historic. When Janet was young, the lawn and the garden were his pride and joy. The grass had to be trimmed precisely a quarter of an inch from the concrete. There could be no weeds. There was a watering schedule to be hewn to precisely. When a neighbor persisted in allowing his dog to toilet on the property, Stratman gathered up the offending evidence in a bag and left it on the man's doorstep.

The interior of the house was eternally in the throes of renovation, the excuse the Cooke females used for not inviting people inside. While his office was an absolute showpiece, and most of the house was tasteful and immaculate, there were always tarps and plaster dust and paint fumes in evidence. One day Stratman completely stripped the upstairs bathroom—fixtures, tiles and all. He left it that way for four years. The entire family was forced to use the small bathroom downstairs. Mornings, Janet and her sister had to arise inordinately early so that they could toilet and dress and eat. The house, by order of Stratman Cooke, had to be returned to a state of orderly quietude for his awakening.

Janet and her younger sister, Nancy, weren't allowed outside their yard, weren't allowed to get dirty, to make noise or to make friends. They were allowed to study, play piano, attend their Catholic church, listen to their parents' extensive collection of classical and opera records, buy and read as many books as they wished. The few fond memories Janet has of her dad have to do with books and the written word. At an early age, Janet got a ribbon from the library for reading the entire children's section; not long after, Stratman marched his daughter into the local bookstore, introduced her to the owner, and set up a charge account in her name. When it came to books, money was no object to him. Every Sunday they'd go to the fountain at the drugstore and read *The New York Times* together. Before she got her malt, Janet had to impress the soda jerk by reading a few paragraphs out loud.

When she started school at the public elementary, Janet remembers, she was "appalled" that none of the other kids—all of them black—were able to read. Her father explained, "These children really can't be your playmates. They are not intellectual enough or well-bred enough for you. Your mother and I have sacrificed too much to let you backslide into their kind of behavior."

"We were very isolated as kids," Janet recalls. "We weren't allowed to invite people over or to go to other people's houses. I think the other children in the neighborhood thought that my sister and I were terrible snobs, and I suppose that by the time we were teenagers, we were. But it didn't start out like that. I think we were both pretty shy. We really didn't know how to act or what to do around other kids. They seemed so wild, so exotic, so unfettered compared to us.

"My father ruled the house with an absolute iron fist. You did not cross him. Everyone in town knew him, though no one knew what he was really like. We were taught, 'What goes on in the house stays in the house.' He was on the city-county planning commission and was always in the newspaper, but nobody was really friends with us. Our family had no relations with any other family. We lived on the block, but that was it. I never could figure out why he wanted to live in an all-black neighborhood if he didn't think the people were good enough for us to associate with. That's the kind of mixed message I grew up with. He was horribly conflicted. It was close to pathological; no, it *was* pathological."

From an early age, Janet was drilled for excellence. To teach her to swim, Stratman threw her into the pool. To the present day, Janet cannot so much as float or dog paddle. Even during summer vacation there were reading lists, book reports, assignments. In second grade, a teacher called to say that Janet was having problems with writing. She frequently reversed her b's and d's, was making other little mistakes that would later be seen as signs of dyslexia. Stratman sat Janet down with a No.2 pencil at the big dining-room table, kept her there until the early hours, pacing back and forth, calling out like a drill sergeant: "Now make a b. Now make a d. Write the word saw. Write the word was."

When her mother finally came downstairs to protest, a huge row ensued. Janet fled to her room. *Why am I so stupid that*

*I can't get this?* she asked herself again and again as her parents battled downstairs—knowing, meanwhile that while it was bad she'd been naughty, it was even worse knowing that her mother was in trouble now too, for sticking up for her. The terror of such times never abated. Later, lying in bed at night, hearing her parents battle, she would dream of moving to Paris, the land of Josephine Baker and James Baldwin. Trying to block the noise, she'd conjugate French verbs out loud, concentrating on her accent, knowing that someday she'd get to France.

By third grade, Janet was enrolled with the children of Toledo's elite in the Maumee Valley Country Day School, one of two black students in her graduating class of forty-three. "I guess it was at Maumee that I first started having this overriding fear that I would never be good enough to do anything. I had fabulous grades, I was a cheerleader, I was a Merit scholar, but I always felt like I was falling just short of the mark.

"Part of that was my father. If we brought home report cards with three As and a B, it was: 'Did anybody get all As?' Nothing was ever good enough to him.

"Over time," Janet says, "I began to feel probably the exact same way my father felt. This stark sense of being alone, of being so out of place, of feeling like some kind of model Negro, the only black face in a white, preppy sea. I had no friends, really. Since we weren't allowed to go out, and since I didn't even have use of a car until senior year, I had to say no every time anybody asked me to do something. Sometimes I said I had to wash my hair. Sometimes I made up these elaborate itineraries for my family, these exotic weekend trips. Then of course I had to stay inside all weekend so no one would find me out. Toledo is a very small town. As you can imagine, after a while, the invitations kind of dried up. None of the sororities would take me, though one of them thought about it one year—they were having this debate about integration. Then they took a Jewish girl instead, and that was deemed sufficient.

"School was just one big pressure after another. I knew I didn't fit in, but I didn't know where I did fit in. I was different, right at the level of the skin, even if the skin was really the only difference. And no matter how many Peter Pan collars and knee socks and lime green sweater sets I wore, I knew I was never going to fit in. The boys couldn't date me. 'Oh god, no!' the parents would say, 'You can't bring a colored girl in my house!' It was very perverse.

"The whole time, I felt this constant pressure to be better than I was, and at all costs. You had to be better than perfect. Your nails had to be perfect, clean and trimmed to a certain length. Your clothes had to be perfect, and only the clothes that he approved. Your grades had to be perfect. You had to have extra credit on top of that. There was no room for anything to go wrong. No room for normal kid stuff. He'd make these lists of things we had to do and read. Never mind what you had to do for school. You had to do that too. He made us memorize the Gettysburg Address. You couldn't just hang out in the yard, you had to do something productive.

"At the same time, I knew deep down that whatever I was able to do, it wasn't going to be good enough. That's what my father taught me, and at this school, I guess, I started to think that maybe he was right."

On that day when the two boys held her down on the bus and covered her with baby powder so she would look the color she acted, the Cooke's reaction, Janet remembers, "was weird. My parents were livid, of course. But there was actually some discussion about whether or not they were going to complain to the headmaster since it was an incident among the black children. To them, it was some kind of racial embarrassment, like maybe it shouldn't be reported because it would underscore the stereotypes. They didn't talk about it for very long, but to me, the fact that this could actually be a question was astonishing. I felt betrayed that my parents didn't just become angry and hop in the car and say, 'We're going to sort this out immediately.' The message they sent was loud and clear. Other people's opinions were more important than their own or their own daughter's. Face, everything was about face. Saving it, preserving it, obscuring it, keeping the best face forward."

Stratman's iron fist created a family that was highly skilled in subversion and deceit. Janet learned from an early age that a well-placed lie could save a lot of trouble. "He had absolute control over the lock on the door," says Janet. "To get out, you had to say where you were going. You couldn't say you were going out with friends or to the movies or to a department store, but you *could* say you were going to the library or a museum or the grocery store. You couldn't buy so much as a skirt or underwear without his approval. My mother and sister and I would buy things and leave them in the trunk of the car until he was gone. Then we'd be in a constant state of terror, worried that he'd notice we were wearing something he hadn't personally approved. There was a lot of dressing at home and then redressing somewhere else. One of us girls had to be home before Dad to get the mail. He'd say, 'Has anyone seen the Lion's department store bill?' And we would all chime in, 'No, Daddy.' Of course, it was in Mother's purse. We used to tease her that she couldn't even go to the bathroom without the thing. Later, after she went into the hospital and my father found out everything, she got herself a P.O. box.

"I've thought about this a lot in the last couple of years," says Janet, sitting on the bench in the mall, checking her watch. "I've thought about lying and how it relates to me, and when I started doing it and why I started doing it, and why, for a long time, it has been more of a red flag for me than it is for most people. The conclusion I've come to is that lying, from a very early age, was the best survival mechanism available to me. And I became very good at it. It was like, do you unleash the wrath of Dad's temper, or do you tell something that is not exactly true and be done with it?

"It is a very twisted way of thinking, I know. Believe me, I know. The problem becomes, what do you do when your worldview is based on such a twisted proposition? What becomes of you?"

She cocks her head coquettishly, throws up her arms, palms high. "Well, I think we know just what becomes of you, now don't we?" says Janet, smiling sadly, her words trailing into a low, sultry, devilish laugh, her trademark, her smoke screen.

Early in her junior year at Maumee Valley, in the hallway at school, Janet spotted her English teacher headed briskly her way. The class had just completed a big essay. *Oh God*, thought Janet. *What did I do?*

"Your paper," said the teacher breathlessly. "It's marvelous! Have you considered going into journalism?"

Janet had always loved words. Not only were books and magazines a plentiful means of escape in the Cooke household; they also formed one of the few grounds on which Janet could stand peacefully with her father. Janet had always been a good writer. When she was eight, her teacher called Mrs. Cooke wondering if someone else had written Janet's book report. While lying to Daddy might have been sanctioned, cheating in school clearly was not. Mrs. Cooke always kept close watch on the girls. She knew everything that Janet and Nancy did. She was positive Janet had written the paper herself. "Maybe she just has talent," Mrs. Cooke suggested.

Following the high school teacher's advice, Janet started keeping a journal. Practically, from that moment, her life began to change. Perhaps, in finding writing and journalism, Janet found a way out. For years it had been assumed Janet's career path would take her to an Ivy League college, a prestigious law school (preferably Harvard) and eventually a place beside her father in his law practice. "It had always been hanging over me, like some kind of eternal damnation, an adulthood working for Daddy."

Now that she had a concrete option, something she could say she really wanted to do, Janet started thinking, *Maybe I can get out of this. Maybe I can do something else. I'm good at it. I'll show him.*

About this time, *Ms.* magazine was founded by Toledo native Gloria Steinem. Janet idolized the feminist icon. "That this girl could come out of Toledo—from much worse material circumstances than I— and have this life that says, 'You don't always have to do what you father or your husband says.' You can't understand the impact. Suddenly, there was light at the end of the tunnel.

"She just gave me all these different ideas. That was the start of my teenage rebellion. From that time on, my father and I fought bitterly. It was open defiance."

Slowly Janet began to rebel. She began to think, *Fuck it, Daddy. I'm going to open the front door. I'm going out with friends. I'm inviting them home. If you don't want to fix the bathroom, fine, you can explain it to them if they have to pee.* For the first time in her life, as if she'd been given some sort of moral press card, Janet began asking the hard questions. "Why do the lights have to be out at a certain hour? Why does the house have to be cleaned in a certain order? Who says we can't go shopping?" The two fought bitterly and often.

"This probably sounds like nothing to people who have been through drugs with their kids, but it was a big thing to me. I left the house. I unlocked the door and just walked out. It was unheard of. But it was sort of like: 'What are you going to do to stop it?' I finally realized that I had some degree of power because of who my father was. The family name was known, he was in the newspaper, he was extremely private. He couldn't afford to have people talking about the horrible, scandalous family life he had, so he couldn't really make a scene in public. I just started doing what I wanted to do.

"I suppose the most perverse manifestation of my rebellion," laughs Janet, "was my inordinate fondness for white boys. The grungier the better. The more pimples, the longer hair, the worse grades. It drove my father crazy. The madder he got, the more boys came around. One time this guy showed up barefoot on a motorcycle, beeped the horn. I ran down the steps, he threw me a helmet. As we pulled off, me waving from on the back with one hand, clinging to him with the other, I could see my mother just about fainting in the doorway. My father was standing in the middle of his hallowed yard, cursing a blue streak. Now *that* had the desired effect."

Feeling as strong as she ever had, Janet went off to college at Vassar, her third choice, behind the University of California, Berkeley, and Smith College.

She hated it immediately. "It was very snotty, very white, very isolated. It was like I'd stumbled into some horrible sorority meeting, sort of like I didn't know how I got in and they didn't know how I got in. Dorm life was a real unpleasant shock. I wasn't used to strangers. I was constipated for the first six weeks—I wasn't going in a bathroom with twenty-five other people. And the food was terrible. Instead of gaining, like most freshman girls, I lost fifteen pounds.

"Work-wise, it was the first time I'd ever been academically challenged. I had to work. I did all right, a three something. But it wasn't like the old days where I could just inhale the book and move along. I really had to push myself. Which was not, fortunately, an unknown concept. The people in my hall didn't have a clue. 'What do I do?' they'd ask, staring at a pile of books. And I would say, 'Did you make notes? Are you going to the library?' I could tell they'd never studied. It was probably one of the few times in my life that I was grateful for the parental boot camp.

"Socially, I was lost. The races were very polarized. There was the black dorm and the black dining table, and if you didn't participate—and I didn't, I thought it was ludicrous—then all the blacks hated you, you didn't have that camp to fall into. So I was pretty lonely. I hung out with a group of hippie intellectuals on my floor. We did things together, but since my dad wasn't giving me any money for expenses—he figured he was paying tuition, books and room and board and that was enough—I couldn't really do the things they wanted to do. I couldn't tell them I didn't have any money—literally, the only money I had was the ten dollars my mother would sneak into a letter now and then. And I wasn't going to borrow money from them. And unless you were a scholarship student, you weren't allowed to get a job. So I just made up excuses—that good ole lying thing again. I mostly just stayed in my room and studied.

"I guess the last straw was just before spring break. I was in this art history class, and we were broken down into our small lecture groups. Our assignment was to pick a work of art over vacation and write about it. And the teacher's going around the room saying, okay, this one's going to Florence, this one's going to Paris. And when I said I was going to Toledo, everybody started laughing. 'You mean Toledo, Spain?' they joked, and I was so humiliated, and it became the big joke for the rest of the semester. I think that's when I decided I wasn't coming back."

That summer of 1973, Janet landed her first newspaper job, an internship at the *Toledo Blade*. She was assigned to the consumer affairs column, called the Zip Line. People would write in and complain about being wronged, and Janet would check it out. Her leverage was the power of the press in a small community. Nobody wanted to be labeled a deadbeat in bold type.

"I didn't see it as a powerful position at first. I wanted to be doing something else, some real reporting. But then, as the summer went on, I realized this was great. They got hundreds of letters. It was hard work, but I liked work, and anyway, considering how hard I'd worked in school all my life, I could go half-speed and still do more than they could print.

"I was in this little office off the city room, and there was this very kindly older guy, a senior reporter, who ran the Zip Line, and a Lou Grant type fellow who was the editor, and I was the girl reporter. I loved the newsroom. I loved the Zip Line, the whole idea of investigating something. I'd go in there and have this carrion-like behavior where I was gonna hunt it down and chew on it until I knew exactly what the situation was. And then I made sure things were put right. It was very gratifying, the first time in my life I ever felt like I was in control."

In the fall, Janet quietly enrolled as a sophomore in the honors program at the University of Toledo. Her mother was an employee of the university; tuition was free. Janet never told her father she wasn't going back to Vassar; her mother didn't bother to mention it. Stratman just realized one day that Janet hadn't left for Vassar, and nothing more was said.

Years later, at a brunch in honor of Janet's sister Nancy's graduation from Brown University, Stratman would give the toast. "I'm sitting here between what might have been (gesturing to Janet) and what is (gesturing to Nancy). So I'd like to propose a toast to my first daughter to graduate from an Ivy League school."

After Janet's graduation from UT, one year prior to her sister's, Janet took a job at the local public television station. By Thanksgiving, she'd moved out of the Cooke's house, into her first apartment. She loved the TV job, even though she was only a glorified secretary, but what she really wanted was to get back to writing, to the *Blade*, where she'd earlier found so much success. Janet called the paper every week and asked if a slot had opened yet. It became a running comic, and very serious ritual between Janet and the editor. After about a year, a staffer in the Living Today section, where Janet had spent her second summer internship, took maternity leave. In the fall of '77, Janet went to work as a full-fledged reporter, filling that slot.

Janet's clips from the *Blade* show a precocious if untrained talent. Some of her stories were written in first person, some were conventionally reportorial, some relied upon unnamed sources. Many concerned issues she'd grown up with—spouse and child abuse, women in the male-dominated workplace, great women to be admired, a series of random pieces decrying the lack of old-fashioned manners in the modern-day world. It was a satisfying beat the *Blade* allowed Janet to carve out for herself. "A lot of this was just coming to the fore at that time. Domestic violence, women's roles, that sort of thing. I was still really interested in things from a Gloria Steinem/feminist perspective. It was hard in the beginning. This being Toledo in '77 and '78, these liberal issues were not easily shoved down the community's throat. But little by little, I was given the go ahead to run with my interests.

"One thing I thought, once I started full time, was that this is gonna cure you of your terminal shyness. Either that, or you're going to have to quit right away. But it turned out that things were really great. It was like, all right, people think I can write, I'm getting paid for it, I'm being forced every day to talk to a new person. And you know what? I was good at it! I did fashion, profiles, interviews, little essays, just about anything. After a while I'd go to the grocery store and write a check, and the cashier would recognize my name from my byline. They'd say, 'Oh yeah, I read that story of yours in Sunday's paper.'

And I was like, 'You did?' You can't imagine how important that was."

In the spring of 1979, a few months before her birthday, Janet began to brood. *My God!* she thought. *I'm almost twenty-five. Am I going to stay in Toledo till I die?*

Janet decided it was time to move on and up. Having just read David Halberstam's, *The Powers that Be*—which didn't help at all in changing her mind about New York being an "uncivilized" place to live—Janet set her sights on the *Washington Post*.

She imagined Washington to be the most cosmopolitan of American cities, a constant whirl of power lunches and politics and parties. And under the tutelage of such luminaries as Bradlee and Woodward, Janet further imagined, she'd become a hard-as-nails, take-no-prisoners journalist "who could dig up a scoop and then write the shit out of it," as Bradlee was known to say. Maybe she'd even end up covering the White House.

Truth be told, she was also looking forward to the men. No more small timers and hayseeds. Just cultured, pedigreed, multilingual hunks, John F. Kennedy crossed with Robert Redford, as he appeared in *All the President's Men*. Perhaps, at some embassy soirée she'd meet a French diplomat and find herself, as she'd imagined as a child, living like a princess in Paris, holding down a slot as the French correspondent for *Elle*.

Janet began reading the *Post* every day. She took books from the library, pulled clips and magazine articles, studied the paper's history, its present. She wrote down bylines that appeared more frequently than others. She investigated their breeding and credentials.

It didn't take long for Janet to realize that her education and experience level were inferior. She went into a funk. What would she do now?

Three days after her twenty-fifth birthday, on July 26, 1980, a broken romance freshly behind her, a new sense of purpose welling inside, Janet sat down at her typewriter to create for herself a new past, a set of credentials that would turn heads at the paper of Bradlee and Woodward.

"My goal," she says, "was to create *Supernigger*."

The meal was served on fine white linen: two salads, two soups, two Cokes. In one chair was Vivian Aplin-Brownlee, thirty-four, a black woman hand-picked by Bradlee himself in the ongoing effort to integrate the newsroom; as the newspaper of the nation's capital, publisher Don Graham felt the *Post* should be among the leaders of the "affirmative action" movement. On the edge of the other chair was Janet Cooke. It was time for her six-month review.

To all appearances, Janet was doing very well at the *Post*; her work was roundly praised. The first story she was assigned was about a youngster who shot a classmate in a public school room. She managed to get a long interview with the doctor; she wasn't able to get to the parents or the kids. Though the editors told her she'd done a great job, she knew she hadn't gotten to the meat of the story, the suspects or victims, though sometimes the best you can do is all you can do, especially in a business that seeks to convince people to spew their guts for public consumption. Janet wondered if the editors' praise was weighted with qualifications—she wondered if they had low expectations because she was young, black and female. And she wondered if they just thought she was incompetent. If they'd only known—it had taken her two hours *just* to find the hospital. She'd told them she had a flat tire.

By mid-February Janet had scored her first big piece, a much discussed takeout on the mood in the 14th Street drug corridor following the assassination of a policeman. Reveling in the reaction among the day-side staff, Janet sent me a note via the internal messaging system, an early form of in-house email: "You should have been here. It was terrific. Graham, Bradlee, flowers, phone calls . . . the works. You are right. I AM spoiled. And if you thought it was bad before . . . By the way, I couldn't get a hotel room in Key West, so I have to go to Nassau (poor me)."

So far at the *Post*, Janet had made a few female friends, all of them white, most of them plain Janes from the Midwest who worked on the paper's large support staff. As for the white men, even though Janet considered them "rude and awkward and poorly dressed," and was forever decrying the sight of so many untucked shirts, saggy pants, and bulging wallet pockets around the newsroom, the men themselves were clearly taken with Janet, tending to babble a bit in her presence. Beauty, elegance, an appearance of chic composure, a sense of humor with a salacious bent—these were not the normal attributes of a modern newspaperwoman, and this fact did not go unnoticed. With Janet in residence, the Weekly section began seeing a host of new visitors dropping by. Publisher Graham bounded through on his way to the company softball game. Ben Bradlee puffed up his chest, paused long enough to launch a few jaunty bons mots, usually in French. Woodward would stand there looking lost, chewing his Beech-Nut furiously. "How are ya?" he'd ask, in his flat Illinois accent.

Janet's most notable issues at the *Post* came under the heading of race relations. None of the African-American staffers or editors much liked her personally, and the feeling was mutual. At a confusing time in the history of race relations, Janet didn't understand—and refused to assume—the militant yet submissive role of the black reporter at the *Washington Post*, an odd position wherein people could feel at once assimilated and estranged. Neither could Janet fathom why a group of some of the most gifted and highly respected men and women in the entire newspaper industry circulated among themselves a humorous, self-deprecating newsletter called "The Mouf." With the legend "Why's our shit so raggedy?" right under the title, and a column headlined "Niggerisms"—which listed faux pas commonly committed by *brothas* and *sistas* in the newsroom—the broadsheet was a rare peek inside the conflicted feelings of the members of the *Post's* minority staffers.

Janet had little, if anything at all besides skin color, in common with the other blacks at the paper, except perhaps for Jane Seaberry, with whom she'd become friends, another Midwestern black woman. Janet's musical tastes tended toward the Rolling Stones, the Who, Steely Dan, opera and classical. She loathed dancing. She dressed like a preppy. Unbeknownst to most, she wore hair extensions and falls, an early adopter of a fad that would later rule in the black community. Once, when black city editor Milton Coleman called her at home on a Sunday, he heard strange noises in the background and asked who was screaming. "That's Carmen, Milt," said Janet, her voice dripping. "I'll go turn her down." When Janet was assigned to cover a Kool and the Gang concert, she bugged her eyes like Pigmeat Markham and said, with the appropriate accent, "Da who and da who? Is dat be sum sorta new colored Mafia?"

Perhaps the oddest aspect of Janet's work was the beat she'd been carving out for herself. This shy, sheltered girl from Toledo was haunting the seedy underbelly of the 14th Street strip, a twenty-four hour drug bazaar about one mile from the White House. Her days of women's issues and essays on manners had become nights of drugs, prostitution, poverty and destitution. On one of her first trips to the ghetto, a kid looked her up and down and asked, "What kinda nigga is you?"

Janet didn't hesitate. "The kind you've never met in your life, young man."

Entranced, the boy ended up giving her a tour of the hood and helping with the story.

This lunch today with Vivian was their fourth meal together. The first had included Stan Hinden; the second two included Coleman. The city editor was tall and ebony complected, a leading member of Washington's young and elite black middle class, the true movers and shakers in a town known to its majority residents at the time as the District of Chocolate; at the time, the population was nearly seventy percent black. Coleman had cut his teeth in the civil rights movement; as a reporter he had covered Marion Barry when the mayor was still wearing dashikis. Later Coleman would become the Metro editor and the reigning black conscience of the newspaper, handpicked by publisher Don Graham. In time Coleman fulfilled his allegiance to the *Post*, revealing that his friend Jesse Jackson, during a private conversation, had referred to New York City as "Hymietown." While the revelation effectively killed Jackson's historic run for the presidency, it sealed Coleman's bond with the *Post*.

Now, at lunch with Vivian, Janet was relieved that Coleman wasn't around. Like most black men, he made her nervous. And, she'd noticed, he tended to talk about people behind their backs for the sake of humor; for instance, he loved lampooning the young black married couple, both assigned to the Weekly, who kept a collection of exotic birds and tended to spend a lot of time at their newly purchased home. "Those niggas have retired," Janet recalls him joking to her. She couldn't help wondering what he was telling people behind *her* back.

At the same time, Janet was not very comfortable with Vivian, either. Relations between the two had never been good. In a sense, Vivian had become the new Stratman in Janet's life, only she proved to be more powerful, mixing as she did her harsh criticisms with fortifying praise, a far more subtle form of manipulation. In any case, as with her father, at the very base of things, Janet felt that nothing she ever did would ever please her boss.

From the moment she'd met Janet, Vivian didn't like her. "I thought her appearance was off-putting—a whole lot of glamour and flash, as opposed to substance," Vivian said by telephone from her home in Washington, D.C., where she lived after quitting journalism. "I would look at her preening at her desk, getting ready to go out in the street and talk to the people. She didn't speak the language. She was hardly useful to me at all."

Vivian speared a forkful of salad and crisply began the evaluation. First, she said, three black male reporters had complained of riding five floors in the elevator with Janet and not hearing so much as "hello." Vivian warned her that she should be nice to these men because they had access to Bradlee, who loved to gossip. If Bradlee should ask the men about Janet, it was in her best interest to make sure they had something interesting to say.

"Of course, girlfriend" Vivian continued, switching to dialect, "you don't wanna let nona those niggas in your panties, you know what I'm sayin? You gots to maintain your image."

Switching back to the King's English, Vivian continued, suggesting that Janet's habit of resting her feet on the desktop had to go. Frequently, she'd been heard hollering across the newsroom like a schoolteacher: "Jan Cooke! Feet on the floor!" Vivian noted that while foot-resting was a favorite pastime of future celebrity sports commentator John Feinstein, who sat nearby and whom Janet had befriended, it was not the image a proud young black woman like herself should project. "Just keep your cotton pickin feet off the desk. Be a lady!"

Vivian went on to suggest that Janet's economy-sized bottle of Maalox should be kept hidden in a drawer, and that making a few black friends around the newsroom might ease the pains in Janet's stomach. "You know, they call you the Ice Princess," Vivian said frankly.

Dumbfounded, Janet pushed away her salad. "What about my work?"

"It's fine. Great. But you need to remember two things. First, no matter how good your last story was, people around here want to know, 'What are you going to do for me today?' Second, no matter how good a writer you think you are, you're nothing without me. I give you assignments. I edit your copy. I push for display. I even have a say in when you're promoted. I've made you what you are, honey pie. I can unmake you just as fast."

My desk in the *Post*'s fifth floor newsroom was near the very front, near the elevator lobby and the entrance to *Style*.

The newsroom warehoused nearly 1,000 smart and ambitious people; I was told it was nearly an acre of space, extending through three different adjoining buildings. At the head of the room was the message center and flanking copy aide station, where all the office supplies were kept and where I'd started my career at the *Post* in the fall of 1978, after an abortive three weeks at Georgetown Law Center. In this era before voice mail and call waiting, employees relied on receptionists to take messages. When you got off the elevator—or even when you got off another phone call—you went directly to the message center, where there were actual physical pages to retrieve, each call logged on a three-by-five inch sheet by one of several vivacious women, placed in an alphabetized rack. My desk was second row center, near the aisle. It was a busy spot, but you got to know everyone.

About noon, my phone rang . . . again. I looked over the top of the desk divider in Janet's direction. The desk she'd temporarily wrangled—she still didn't have one of her own—was all the way down the center aisle, on the other side of the room, back in the Weekly section, hard against the aquarium-like glass offices occupied by Woodward, his deputy David Maraniss, and the columnist Richard Cohen. Starting time for most reporters was basically 10 a.m. This was probably the fifth time Janet had called in the past two hours. The previous four calls had ended with me walking back to her desk to look at the story that was growing on her screen. Standing at her place with the phone to her ear, Janet caught my eye and waved discreetly. There was a crooked smile on her face, half apology, half mischief. And those huge brown eyes. She had a way about her. She pulled you in.

"Can't you please just transfer the story to my terminal?" I cajoled. "Like I *just* showed you?" We were engaged in a somewhat complicated, on-again-off-again interoffice romance. "Fishing off the company pier," as Bradlee was known to call it, was expressly forbidden. All this back and forth was definitely not cool.

"But I keep forgetting how."

"I'll talk you through it. First you have to define..."

Seven months earlier, back in February, when Janet had written the note to me about her 14th Street piece and all the kudos she'd received, there had been another paragraph appended. "Listen," it said, "thanks for letting me bother you. I probably never would have finished the story if you hadn't been around."

That was the root of our relationship. I was her boyfriend, her lover, her friend, her sometime-enemy. But most of all, I was her editor.

It began quite naturally. After about a year as a copy boy, during which time I worked in the wire room at night and freelanced stories during the day, I'd received a promotion from Woodward, a staff job as the night police reporter.

When Janet arrived, I'd only just been given a desk of my own. I worked the night shift, seven until three in the morning. Some nights I'd be stationed in my office at police headquarters; some nights I'd be out chasing stories. And some nights I stayed in the office and monitored the police and fire districts from there. In between calls I'd roam the nearly empty newsroom, waiting for a proper disaster or crime, something that would give me license to hustle out, mount up, and go play reporter. Many nights on my newsroom wanderings I'd encounter Janet, sitting alone in the Weekly section, bathed in the sickly green light of her terminal, gulping Maalox, laboring to bring a story to life on her screen. She was tall and beautiful and so clever in repartee that she made me feel like I was in a movie written by Nora Ephron. I offered what help I could; it wasn't long before I was invited to sit down at her keyboard and take a look at her piece. From there, I guess you could say, I edited my way into her affections.

As a couple we had both chemistry and geography in our favor; our apartments were barely two blocks apart. My "English basement" was on a leafy side street, around the corner from the Duke Ellington Bridge. Janet's was a lovely restored building right on Columbia Road, just at the gateway to Adams Morgan, which at the time was beginning to blossom into its period as Washington's hip new night district. Her third-floor one bedroom was an astronomical seeming $750 a month—mauve wall-to-wall carpeting, cherry wainscoting, delightful central air. Ours was both an intense and stormy relationship. At work and at play, there was no lack of drama. We felt very alive.

In late July, Janet started researching a story about a new type of heroin that supposedly caused the user's skin to ulcerate. It came from the Golden Triangle of Asia. The word on the street was the police were planning to relax enforcement on smuggling and sales because they expected racial unrest in the city during the hot summer that was upon us. Because it was a big story, and because Vivian had slated all of August for vacation, Janet was assigned to Coleman and the Metro desk for the duration of her work on the piece. She was overjoyed.

"I would have done anything to get away from Vivian," says Janet. "If they would have said, 'We'll get you away from Vivian, but you're going to have to sit at a desk out on 15th Street,' I would have said, 'Can I start tomorrow?' Things were just vicious with her, and I never knew why. I didn't want her job. I didn't want her man. I didn't want her life. Why did she hate me so?" With a little luck, Janet figured, she could make a big hit with this story and effect herself a transfer to Metro. It was all she wanted. To be part of the "real staff."

Janet worked on the story for weeks. Library books and research journals and notes piled up high on her borrowed desk. At one point Janet landed an interview with an official of Howard University's drug abuse program. Sitting in were two community outreach workers.

During the interview, while the official was out of the room and Janet was still questioning the outreach workers, the subject of their conversation turned to the ages of the various addicts they'd seen and treated.

"There's even an eight-year-old who's being treated at RAP [a residential drug-treatment facility]," one of the workers said.

Janet's ears pricked up, but she acted cool, continuing the general interview, doubling back now and then to the boy. But they wouldn't give her his name.

When Janet got back to the newsroom, she excitedly told Coleman about the boy. Coleman was ecstatic. "That's a fuckin' front-page story!" he said. "You've got to find that kid!"

Janet called the outreach program at RAP. The director denied having any such patient.

For the next eight weeks, Janet searched frantically for the boy, doing everything a reporter could think to do.

At one point, I was in her apartment when she had a phone conversation with a social work administrator. Listening to only one side of the conversation—no speaker phones in homes in those days— it seemed to me there may have actually been such a boy somewhere in the city. I listened as Janet worked to confirm the existence of the boy. Then I listened as she seemed to get confirmation, and moved on to trying to set a meeting of some sort. Eventually she began to plead, as reporters will sometimes do. She'd been working so hard for so long. She just needed a break from somebody. But I cannot confirm that there was anyone on the other side of the call. If there wasn't, it was a hell of a performance; later I would find out the truth.

Eventually Janet went to Coleman and explained she couldn't find the kid. The administrator wouldn't divulge the boy's identity. What was she supposed to do? Coleman excused himself and went to see the *Post's* managing editor, Howard Simons. When he returned, Coleman told Janet, "OK, it's set. Tell them we don't need to know their names." The paper was willing to publish the story anonymously—they'd stand behind the first amendment and protect the identity of their sources. Like Woodward and Bernstein before her, the *Washington Post* had her back.

Janet returned to work.

Days passed.

No word.

Vivian returned after Labor Day. The first thing she did was march over to Coleman and ask about Janet's progress. She summoned Janet, asked why she hadn't finished the story yet. Janet explained that she couldn't get to the child. In a rare moment of public weakness, Janet confessed to the older woman that she didn't think she'd *ever* find the boy.

"Well, find another boy," Vivian said. "You can't give up. "That's a front-page story. And I can't give you much more time. It's make or break, girlfriend. Get to it."

Janet went back to her borrowed desk and pretended to dial a call. She let her long hair fall around her heavily made-up face, hiding her tears. She felt like an utter failure. She was so disappointed. She'd spent so much time on the project, and now it was falling apart. She'd never get away from Vivian, never get to Metro. She'd be a laughingstock. She'd be fired.

Two possibilities presented themselves. One: She could go to a senior editor on the paper, maybe Bradlee, and say that she couldn't work under the conditions to which she was being subjected by Vivian and Coleman.

Two: She could resign.

Neither, she realized, was tenable.

The lower she sank, the worse she felt, the more she started thinking about one thing: "I kept hearing Milton telling me to offer them total anonymity in return for their story. At some point, it dawned on me that that no one would have to know who they were. Probably not even my editors. The idea that I could simply make it all up, that I could weave what I imagined all these people to be like into the factual information I already had researched about heroin... it just kept drifting in and out of my head.

"From there, it became this tug of war with my conscience. How could I write what I knew wasn't true? It was the worst sin in journalism. But I was reasonably certain that the child existed, and I had seen, firsthand, some of the destruction that heroin was capable of causing. And I was desperate. Utterly desperate. People have always tried to say I was motivated by ambition, celebrity, notoriety, prizes. Well let me say this: What I was motivated by was panic, depression and fear.

"I don't know what happened. I was out of my mind, I guess. Maybe I went a little crazy. I just sat down and wrote the whole thing, top to bottom."

And so it was that I'd been awoken at midnight on my night off by a telephone call.

"I found the kid," Janet told me. "His name is Tyrone."

Details flowing like tears, tears like details, she poured out her tale.

Tyrone lived in a dreadful part of town. When she'd gotten out of her sporty, green metallic 240Z, she said, men hanging around the street corners whistled and yelled obscenities. Distracted, she almost locked her keys inside—luckily the passenger door was still open. She interviewed the boy and his mom. All around her in this creepy but well-appointed house was a rotating cast of skeletal junkies, people cooking spoons of heroin, tying off, firing up. Toward the end of the evening, Janet told me, she watched Ron—a dealer and the mom's boyfriend—give the boy his shot of heroin. Such a beautiful little kid, Janet lamented. So wizened. So lost. Little freckles over the bridge of his nose. The biggest, velvety brown eyes she'd ever seen. And a tiny striped Izod T-shirt. She just wanted to give him a hug. It seemed like he needed it. It was interesting, she also noted, how smoothly a needle could pierce the skin, sliding in so easily, like a straw into the center of a freshly baked cake.

The boy, she said, had received his shot with glee, smiling wanly and nodding out.

And after that, Ron picked up a butcher knife: "If I see any police, Miss Lady," Janet told me he'd threatened, "me and my knife will be around to see you."

Janet fled the house. Outside, she said, she vomited.

On the other end of the phone, she broke down—a wailing, strangled cry. I tried to comfort her.

A few minutes passed. Janet settled and switched gears. "Would you mind going over some of this stuff with me?" she asked. In the background I could hear the rustle of notes—she'd gathered hundreds of pages since her work had begun. She read me some quotes, wanted to know which I thought were the strongest. Then she wanted to talk about structure, about how to weave the Tyrone stuff in with all she knew about the potent, skin-ulcerating, hot summer heroin that had been the original subject of her research.

As she chattered on, happily engaged in her work—sounding perhaps more in control and confident than I'd ever heard—I kept thinking:

*Didn't I see her car when I drove past her apartment two hours ago?*

After forty-five minutes of shop talk, Janet began to sob again. "I'm so scared."

"You want me to come over?"

"Just for a little while?"

The next morning, Janet came to work early. She told Coleman the great news. He told her to write it strong, like a Coltrane song, and sent her to her keyboard. What he didn't know was that she'd brought with her to work a fourteen-page, typewritten draft of the completed story.

By noon Janet was "finished" with her piece. This was the second development that felt wrong. Each time I'd been summoned to her desk, another big chunk of story had appeared on the screen. This was not her way. Stories usually came to Janet slowly and painfully, word by word, line by line. There was always a lot of deleting and restarting. The process often took days or weeks.

But not this time. When I instructed her how to transfer the story to my terminal—creating when she did an electronic record of my possession of the story and the editing changes

I would make—the piece was all there in finished form, start to finish.

*Jimmy is eight years old and a third-generation heroin addict, a precocious little boy with sandy hair, velvety brown eyes and needle marks freckling the baby-smooth skin of his thin brown arms.*

*He nestles in a large, beige reclining chair in the living room of his comfortably furnished home in Southeast Washington. There is an almost cherubic expression on his small, round face as he talks about life—clothes, money, the Baltimore Orioles.*

The story continues for 2,000 words. At one point, Jimmy—the name Janet chose to substitute for the original Tyrone (an improbable choice that would later seem somewhat racist)—begins twisting uncomfortably in his chair, needing his fix. Ron enters with a syringe, calls the boy over.

*He grabs Jimmy's left arm just above the elbows, his massive hand tightly encircling the child's small limb. The needle slides into the boy's soft skin like a straw pushed into the center of a freshly baked cake. Liquid ebbs out of the syringe, replaced by bright red blood. The blood is then reinjected into the child. . . .*

*"Pretty soon, man," Ron says, "you got to learn how to do this for yourself."*

I made a few changes, transferred the piece back to Janet. Then I picked up the phone and called her extension.

"I think you may have just won yourself a Pulitzer, Ms. Cooke."

"Maybe now they'll find me a desk," she said, laughing.

Late Friday evening, September 26, most of the day side had gone home; the newsroom was virtually empty, except for the skeleton crew of night staff, to which I belonged. Coleman sat

Janet by his desk, in the chair reserved for the reporter of the moment—sometimes a hot seat, sometimes a throne.

"Now listen," Janet remembers Coleman telling her. He looked straight into her eyes. She found it difficult to hold his gaze; she was unsure what he was getting ready to tell her. By tonight, she thought, the story would be set in type. By tomorrow, everything would be over. *What now?* she wondered. *Have they found me out?* So far, there'd been no indication of that at all. Around the newsroom, the brass had been treating her like Princess Diana. She concentrated on Coleman's bushy moustache, determined not even to blink.

"You have written a story that is certain to be controversial. You have seen a crime and you may be subpoenaed. We don't think so, but you may. You should know that the *Post* will stand behind you 100 percent. If you are subpoenaed, and you refuse to reveal your sources, you may be found in contempt of court and have to spend time in jail."

Coleman let the information sink in for a long beat. "Before the story goes," he concluded, "if you don't want to face that, we won't run it. Think it over. Tell me in the morning."

Janet thought about it all night. In her mind, jail was nothing compared to the emotional roller coaster of the past few months. At this point, she would have been happy to go; jail would have been a relief. Anything to take her away from the office and this impossible situation she knew she'd gotten herself into. In one way, she still thought the story would take care of her troubles once and for all. But she also knew in the back of her mind that the publishing of "Jimmy's World" could set in motion consequences so severe she didn't even want to think about them.

The next morning, Saturday, she came in bright and early.

"Let it go," she told Coleman, her chin held high.

The presses began rolling at 9:54 p.m., Saturday, September 27, 1980. The Post circulated almost 900,000 copies of the paper. Additionally, the story was wired to 300 news outlets in the U.S. and around the world via the *Washington Post-LA Times* News Service.

By the next day, scores of millions of people were talking about "Jimmy's World" and Janet Cooke. "The switchboard lit up like a space-launch control room," according to an 18,000-word internal investigation, authored by *Post* ombudsman Bill Green, published by the *Post* after Cooke's Pulitzer scandal was revealed.

Green continued: "'Jimmy' never existed, but his story convulsed the city and humiliated the *Washington Post*—proud house of Watergate investigations . . . Jimmy's story struck at Washington's heart. They (the residents of Washington) called the story racist and criminal. They voiced concern about the boy. That was the central question, echoed around the world: 'What about the boy?'"

From a journalist's point of view, "Jimmy's World" was a home run, the kind of article Metro editor Woodward would call a "Holy shit!" story, a piece that took your breath away, the most precious coin of the realm. But to readers in an overwhelmingly African-American town, "Jimmy's World" was a clear example of exploitation, headlines before humanity. Because Janet had supposedly offered a promise of anonymity to "Tyrone" and his family in exchange for access to their story, the *Post*'s editors were forced to refuse to give city officials any help to locate the boy and bring the parents to justice. Though the *Post*'s editors believed they were acting within the sacred bonds of the First Amendment, readers were not so sure. They wondered: How could this great liberal newspaper, known for bringing down a president, write about this poor child (and make money from his story) and then keep him hidden? Clearly he was being abused.

On Monday morning, D.C. police launched a massive, citywide search. A $10,000 reward was offered. On Tuesday Mayor Barry announced that officials knew who Jimmy was and that he was in treatment. Then Barry's office retracted his statement. Later the police would halt the search, calling the story a hoax.

By the following weekend, wrote ombudsman Green, Coleman was beginning to feel uneasy. At first he had bought Janet's story without question. The details, he concluded, were solid. Those parts about the needle: like a straw into a freshly baked cake. How could an innocent Oreo cookie like Janet fabricate that sort of thing, such a telling detail? According to Green, Coleman established an eleven-member task force to follow up Janet's story. Five were to follow the breaking news—the progress of the police search, the response from the city and the world. The remaining six were assigned a very specific task: find another Jimmy. With so many questions about the veracity of the story, editorial logic held that finding another case would put to rest the doubts.

Likewise, Watergate hero Bob Woodward had signed off on the piece. Woodward told Green that the way he saw things, stories are divided into two types, "those carrying possible libel or criminal charges and all others." As Jimmy was anonymous, Woodward said he believed the story fell into category two. Woodward would also tell Green that he thought it odd that Janet had written a very complicated story in an inordinately short period of time. "In a way," Woodward told Green, "both she and the story were almost too good to be true... (But) the story was so well-written and tied together that my alarm bells simply didn't go off. My skepticism left me."

One vocal doubter was the streetwise black reporter Courtland Milloy. He was teamed with Janet on a follow-up story, and they drove around Jimmy's neighborhood together. Milloy told Green, "It didn't take long to see that she didn't know the area. It's one of the toughest sections in town... She said she didn't see the house. I asked her if it was to the right of us, the left of us, or had we passed it. She didn't know."

Milloy had the suave demeanor of his New Orleans roots; from the beginning Janet never liked him or his "peacock strut." She remembers: "We drove around and Courtland kept stopping every ten minutes to go to the bathroom, to buy chips, to buy a drink. Ostensibly, we were looking for another Jimmy, but it soon became clear that Courtland had been assigned to trick me into leading him to Jimmy's house. I remember saying, 'Well, you know, it was dark and I don't remember exactly which house it was.' We spent the whole day out there, him grilling me without trying to seem like he was grilling me. Like I was so stupid or inexperienced that I wouldn't recognize the most basic, stupid reporter trick.

"I came back to the office saying to myself, *Well, they think they know something, but they're just fishing.* So I thought, *The best defense is a good offense: I'm just gonna get in Milt's face about this, very vocally and very immediately, and I'll make these doubts go away.*

"I marched right up to Milt and said, 'What the fuck was that all about?' I said it at a pretty decent decibel level, with a tone of total outrage. And you know, my mother was right, it really does pay to be a lady most of the time, because when you have to turn around and be the other thing, I tell you, people pay attention. I yelled at him and told him I didn't appreciate this sort of treatment, and I went on and on, and then I stormed off to the woman's john. After a while, a long while, they sent Jane Seaberry in to see if I was okay. Nobody said anything after that."

Vivian was also skeptical. She told Green: "I never believed it, and I told Milton (Coleman) that. . . In her eagerness to make a name for herself, Janet would often write farther than the truth would allow. When challenged on facts in other stories, Janet would reverse herself, but without dismay or consternation. I knew she would be tremendously out of place in a shooting gallery. I didn't believe she could get access."

Later, on the day Janet's Pulitzer was announced, Vivian told Green, she went to Coleman and said, "I hope she has committed the perfect crime."

Meanwhile, Janet was in a state: "I was astonished by the attention I got. I was uncomfortable. I just wanted it to go away. It was a real lesson for me, in a lot of ways. It was a lesson about the power of what you write. Not so much the power of the press, but that, you know, people really do read the newspaper and don't just put it in the bottom of the birdcage. And I realized that people out there, the readers, weren't as shitty and misanthropic as you come to believe. The shitty and misanthropic ones are the journalists themselves. Reporters really do have this attitude that they are in a room full of people who know more than anyone else, who are better than everyone else. They think only they know what's important and who's important and which world view is true. Let's face it. You get warped in a business where death lands you on A1 and thirty injuries gets C6. There's a bus crash and you keep calling the hospital. 'Did anyone die yet?' Because the minute someone dies, the story's value goes way up. The more gloom, the more doom, the higher the profile, the more play. The worse it is, the better it is.

"Out in the real world, everybody was saying, 'How can we help the kid?' I felt horrible about that. Really ashamed. I had taken these people for an incredibly emotional ride. I got letters saying, 'Oh, your story made me cry. How can I help? I have an extra bedroom.'"

One night Janet and I were at a concert at the Warner Theatre, sitting in the balcony. Some time had passed; it was March of 1981. The band we'd come to see was one of Janet's favorites.

She was so excited, in fact, that we'd showed up at the theater a week too early, only to discover a different act on the marquee.

Now we were back on the correct night. The group was called Chicken Legs, a bunch of skinny white guys with long hair and big amplifiers. Once again, the last place you'd ever expect to find a woman who looked like Janet.

Midway into the show, the group struck up their anthem. Rockets burst. Lasers strafed the crowd. The lead guitarist jumped off the stage, commenced a Chuck Berry duck-walk up the center aisle, playing a hot solo.

"I want more attention from you," Janet was complaining. "But we broke up seven months ago," I said. "I'm supposed to be just a friend. A friend with benefits. Not your boyfriend. Wasn't that the agreement?"

The guitar wailed. Janet began to cry.

I didn't know what to do. I was pretty young. She was pretty troubled. It had been a long and emotional ride. "When will you ever be happy?" I hollered over the music and the crowd noise. "What do you want?"

Just at that moment, the song reached a crescendo. The audience rose, cheering, a standing ovation.

Janet stood, too. She stretched her arms out over the applause, as if to catch it, a lover in a field of daisies. "This," she said. "I want *this*." Her eyes fluttered, slowly closed. The look on her face was pure bliss.

This was Janet's world between the publication of the story and the announcement of the Pulitzer Prize winners in April. She went to work each day, appeared busy as ever. She was finally given a desk in Metro. As it happened the desk she was given was in my row. Two down, opposite side. I faced the Weekly. She faced the message center. Patrick Tyler, Pete Earley, Keith Richburg, Tom Morgan. As in every row in the joint, the egg-shaped desk chairs were occupied by people who would make important contributions to their chosen profession. Janet was at once relieved and awed. *You must do everything twice as well as everyone else. There is no room for fucking up. There is no slack.* She wrote a few stories, mostly day stuff as assigned. Top-most in her mind was finding another Jimmy. She needed another Jimmy. She had to have another Jimmy. *But what have you done for me today?* After the Pulitzer nominations were posted in December, she appeared functional to most. *Be cleaner than clean. More polite than polite. Put your best face forward.* Those few who knew her well could see otherwise.

She lived on a diet of Dexatrim, vitamins, Coca-Cola and chocolate. Being of African-American descent, Janet possessed a prominent rear end, a little bit of junk in the trunk, roundly admired—by everyone except Janet. In many ways, Janet was what she was sometimes accused of being, black on the outside, somewhat white-identifying on the inside. When she looked in the mirror, she never found exactly what she was hoping to see. She tried different diets. She shopped incessantly, mostly at Bloomingdales, trying to find something she liked herself wearing. It is interesting to note that she never had any trouble navigating the fifteen miles to White Flint Mall, in the Maryland suburbs.

As 1981 continued, Janet stopped opening her mail, which was mostly overdue bills. Her apartment was a mess, old newspapers and balled-up clothes strewn about. She would become frightened when the telephone rang. She developed insomnia and migraines. As a tonic, she drank Jack Daniel's or Dewar's. She called me one night to say she'd swallowed a whole bottle of Valium. When I got there, she confessed she'd lied. She called another night to say she was about to bleach her hair blonde. She called some nights every hour on the hour. Once she drove over and looked in my window, braving a dark alley and a set of basement stairs to see into my bedroom. She called from a pay phone, asking, "Are you done with that slut yet?"

She banged on my front door at four in the morning to tell me she never wanted to see my face again.

She said she was going to a shrink; at the appointment hour, she'd be spotted at Bloomingdale's. She was always late but always had an elaborate excuse. After missing dinner at a reporter's parent's house, Janet arrived in time for dessert with a harrowing story: She'd been walking down her hallway on the way to her car when she heard something scratching on a door. She opened the door, she said, and found a man on the floor, having a heart attack. She administered CPR until the ambulance came. Most probably, she'd spent the last few hours in her bedroom, in front of the closet and the full length mirror, trying on different outfits, taking them off, trying to find something she liked herself wearing, creating a huge pile on the floor.

Though she was making about $27,000 a year, Janet's finances were a disaster. She was maxed out on her gas card, close to the edge on the others. In December, realizing she could no longer afford her own apartment, she moved into the exclusive and fashionable Ontario Apartments, the setting for Nora Ephron's book and movie *Heartburn*, based on the author's relationship with her former husband, Woodward's Watergate partner, Carl Bernstein. Bernstein still lived in the building. Janet's roommate at the Ontario was Elsa Walsh, a young reporter who'd recently begun dating Woodward.

While a number of couples hooked up at the *Post*, employee relationships were strictly taboo. Woodward was a manager; he wasn't encouraged to date his employees. Some nights, Janet was pressed into service as the couple's beard. They'd go to dinner with one of Woodward's male friends, trying to make it appear to be a group outing, just a bunch of reporters having a meal. "Here was a guy who's my boss and wouldn't give me the time of day anymore, unless it's about something official, and in my off hours I get rounded up to go out with him and my roommate so they can look longingly at each other across the wine glasses and I can sit there making small talk, feeling like an idiot. I was trying to be a good Joe, but it was very stressful."

Likely, Janet also felt guilty. Her check for her portion of the apartment deposit bounced, and she was having trouble meeting her half of the expenses. Likely, she was into Walsh for quite a few bucks. Plus, dinners with Woodward were always free.

At work, the pressure to come up with another fabulous tale led Janet to the story of a fourteen-year-old prostitute. This time Coleman insisted on meeting the girl. Lunches with the prostitute and her pimp were scheduled, rescheduled, canceled. The story didn't run. Some editors asked why. Did this mean Coleman didn't believe Janet? Did he now think that "Jimmy" was a hoax? If so, why had the story been nominated for a Pulitzer?

"I began to realize," Janet says, "that I needed to be doing something else. I felt like I was falling into this kind of emotional and financial and moral hole that I needed to figure a way out of. I started to really think about quitting.

I figured, I could always go home. They'd find a desk for me at the *Blade* in short order, I was sure of that. Or I thought, maybe I can go somewhere else. It's not like I didn't have any clips. I was a *Post* reporter.

"But that was the thing. If I walked away, I was walking away a colossal failure. It was like, 'You're going to leave the *Washington Post*? Break the golden handcuffs?' That seemed impossible. It just felt like college all over again, only the *Post* was a much bigger deal than Vassar. It never occurred to me that if it wasn't right for me it didn't matter, that people had done it before, did it all the time. I had no sense of, you know, you've got to save yourself first. You've got to think about your sanity. You've got to think about your well-being. None of that was important to me at the time. I know everybody now says it was a case of no self-esteem or no self-respect, and I think that maybe that has become a sort of fashionable excuse. But in my particular case, I know it is the reason for quite a lot of things.

"I had huge phone bills," she continues. "I'd call my mother and just cry on the phone for an hour. And she was like, 'Sweetie, you have every reason to be happy. You have a beautiful apartment, a great job, a nice roommate. You've been nominated for a Pulitzer Prize, for Heaven's sake!'

"I couldn't say, 'I'm drowning here. I'm lonesome. I've really fucked up bad.' I mean, for the first time in my life, my father acted like he was actually proud of me. How could I tell them what had happened?"

On the afternoon of April 3, the telephone in Janet's hotel room rang. President Ronald Reagan days earlier had been shot by a man who said he'd done it to gain the affections of the actress Jodie Foster, a student at Yale at the time. Janet was sent to New Haven—a testament, clearly, to her ability to hide her inner turmoil. It was considered a privilege, a prized gig, for a Metro reporter to be sent anywhere out of town. Obviously, the higher ups had no clue what was going on with Janet.

It was Coleman on the line. "Are you sitting down?" he asked.

"No. Why?"

"Well, the Pulitzers were announced today."

"Yes, so, what are you saying? Stop beating around the bush!"

"You *won*."

Janet began to laugh. She giggled uncontrollably. Almost hysterically. She really thought he was joking. She'd never won anything in her life, despite what her resume said. "What are you really calling about?"

"Jesus Christ, Janet," Coleman said. "You won the fucking Pulitzer Prize for feature writing. Here. Let Bradlee tell you."

As Ben Bradlee took the line, Janet's hands and feet went cold and she broke out in a sweat. She sat down on the bed.

*Well*, she thought, *my life is over.*

"Say two words in Portuguese," Ben Bradlee challenged.

Janet shrugged.

"Do you have any Italian?"

"No."

Bradlee sighed heavily. "If you had to speak French to me right now to save your job, what would you say?"

Actually, Janet *could* speak French. All those nights as a girl, lying in bed, conjugating verbs, dreaming of Paris, trying to block out the noise of her parents' fights. Years later, after this conversation was made public in Ombudsman Green's report, Janet would run into her French teacher from Maumee Valley. "You were my best student," she would say. "Why couldn't you manage a simple sentence?"

As she stood before Bradlee, seated in his big chair, in his office with the big windows looking out on the bustling newsroom, something came over Janet and she dug in her heels. She was done jumping through hoops, she suddenly decided. It was an odd time to be making new rules, but she didn't have any control. Four French words echoed in her mind. They translated, "Go fuck yourself." When she attempted to say something else, the sentence came out a garbled word salad. Woodward and Coleman and the others in the room snorted their disapproval.

In the end, it was the résumé that got her.

Supernigger fell to earth.

The Pulitzers were announced publicly on April 13. The *Toledo Blade*, proud of its former employee, prepared a story. It went to press at 8 a.m.

Later that morning, Ombudsman Green wrote in his investigation, *Blade* editors read the biographical sketches of the Pulitzer winners that moved over the AP wire. The sketches were based on the résumés submitted with the entries. The *Blade's* bio for Janet, taken from its personnel records, differed considerably. Blade editors alerted the wire service.

By afternoon an AP reporter called Janet. She stood by her Pulitzer bio. What no one had yet realized was that her Pulitzer bio differed from her first fake résumé, the one she had created when applying to the *Post*. For the Pulitzers, she had added two more languages, a year at the Sorbonne and six more writing awards.

Sometime after three in the afternoon, Bradlee and managing editor Simons received simultaneous phone calls. An AP editor wanted Simons. The assistant to the president of Vassar wanted Bradlee. Both callers were asking about Janet's résumé.

"Take her to the woodshed," Bradlee ordered. For the next eleven hours—in various offices and conference rooms at the *Post*, in the Capitol Hilton bar, and even in Coleman's car, as the two drove around southeast, looking for Jimmy's house—Janet was interrogated, cajoled, comforted, pressured, flattered, put on the spot by Bradlee, Woodward, Simons, Coleman and others. They were some of the best journalists in the world. One by one, Janet admitted to the false résumé items.

But she drew the line at Jimmy. The story, she kept insisting, was true.

At 11:30 p.m., according to Green, Coleman and Janet joined Woodward, his deputy David Maraniss, and assistant managing editor for personnel, Tom Wilkinson, in the fifth-floor conference room. Janet says she has little recollection of the events. The quotes that follow come from Green.

David Maraniss was cast as the good cop, as he was every day. He was known to his staff as "a real human being," a delicate writer and caring family man who would later go back to writing and win the Pulitzer himself. Janet loved David. Everyone loved David. He had soulful, droopy eyes; he listened; he really seemed to care.

Woodward played the bad cop. "It's all over," he said to her. You've got to come clean. Your notes show us the story is wrong. We can show you point by point how you concocted it . . . It might be a brilliant fake, but it's a fake."

"This is getting too cruel," Janet said, sobbing. "All I have left is my story."

"Give up the Pulitzer, and you can have yourself back," Maraniss said.

"If a just God were looking down," Woodward asked, "what would he say is the truth?"

"I don't know what you mean," Janet said coldly. God and Woodward and everyone else paled in the face of her father, Stratman. This was nothing compared to the wrath she'd felt from him as a girl.

Eventually, Woodward gave up. He, Coleman and Wilkinson left the room. Maraniss took a seat next to Janet. She began to weep. A deft writer who himself was no stranger to newsroom drama, Maraniss started crying, too.

"The first time I saw you today I thought, *Oh boy, he knows, and I'm going to have to tell him*," Janet said. "I couldn't lie to you. I couldn't tell them. I never would tell Woodward. The more he yelled, the more stubborn I was. Wilkinson represents the corporation. It means so much to Milton. You guys are smart. Woodward for the mind, you for the heart—why are you smiling?"

"Because I had a tremendous surge of empathy for you, refusing to submit to the institution in an absurd situation. You were so strong not to give in. The institution will survive."

"Oh, David," Janet sighed. "What am I going to do?"

"You can recover and you will," Maraniss said.

They talked for a while, exchanging intimacies. Then, at 1:45 a.m., Maraniss told Green, he said to Janet, "You don't have to say anything to the others. I'll do it for you. What do I tell them?"

Janet swallowed. "There is no Jimmy and no family. It was a fabrication. I want to give the prize back."

Just then, Woodward, Coleman and Wilkinson returned to the room. Looking up from his seat next to Janet, his eyes still red, his nose a little stuffy, David announced, "You can go home now, Jimmy is a composite."

Then, according to Green, each editor hugged and kissed Janet.

"I'm sorry I was such a son of a bitch," said Woodward.

"I deserved it," Janet answered.

"Yes you did," Woodward said.

Green's section on the "confession" ends like this:

"Cooke's mother arrived from Toledo Wednesday (the next day), and her father flew to Washington Friday. While Janet Cooke was being grilled by *Washington Post* editors, her father had spent the night of April 14th filling out his income tax returns.

"What did I do that went wrong?" Stratman Cooke asked. "She was extremely ambitious, eager to prove herself. I encouraged that."

A few days later, I returned from Europe. The next afternoon, a Saturday, my doorbell rang. It was Janet. Ever the dogged investigator, she'd managed to wrangle my date and time of arrival from the airline.

Though I was unaware, after the roof caved in on Janet, the *Post* had been hunting me across England and the Continent, where I'd gone to visit some friends and, honestly, to get away from Janet for a while. Reporter Tom Sherwood, one of my first mentors at the *Post*, actually tracked my parents down to the surgical recovery room at Sinai Hospital in Baltimore, where—also unbeknownst to me—my father had just undergone a disc operation. In those days before cell phones and email, when you paid for stuff with traveler's cheques, it was easier to be out of touch. Sherwood did discover that I'd paid a visit to future *Post* executive editor Len Downie at the *Post's* London bureau office, but my trail went cold after that. (He didn't think to check the Bulldog, my favorite hash bar in Amsterdam, where I had gone for my last days of rest and recovery).

Of course, I knew nothing of the drama that had transpired between Janet and the newspaper's top brass. Janet seemed visibly different, more sedate; clearly, a burden had been lifted. Her long ringlets were gone; her hair was cut into a short Afro and she was wearing boyish, baggy clothes. We sat on my couch and she recounted the events. She was pissed, she said, that David didn't let her write her own letter of resignation, even though Ombudsman Bill Green would later say she did.

"Be careful," she warned. "They're trying to pin this on you, too. They want to say you collaborated. They have that edit trail thingy, that record from the computer. It shows I transferred it to you and that you edited what I wrote."

I thanked her. We had a good cry, a lingering hug. Maybe something more. Our relationship was always like that. Then we said goodbye.

The next morning was my first day back to work, a quiet Sunday day shift. I was, after all, a kid playing with the grownups.

Maybe I was precocious, maybe I thought I was smart or intuitive enough to predict this whole thing, but I was still only twenty-four. I guess you could say I had the naivete of the innocent. I had no idea about the shit storm that was coming.

The moment the elevator doors opened and I walked into the newsroom, a woman editor approached me, followed me to my desk, and pulled up a chair. She was no one of power, no one of particular note. She was not even close to being in the loop—a copy editor on the national side stuck with early Sunday morning duty. But it didn't matter. She was a journalist, a *Washington Post* journalist. She wanted to know what I knew. *What's the gossip?* This clearly was it.

Over the next couple of weeks—besides my official interviews with Woodward, Coleman and the other brass that would soon follow—I'd be holding scores of similar impromptu press conferences around the newsroom. Of course I answered every question I was asked as truthfully as I could. For a while there it got a little scary. Imagine being twenty-four and being interrogated over a two-day period by Bob Woodward. Luckily in this case, the truth was my best defense.

Almost every time I was questioned, I ended up telling the story about the time Janet and I traveled to the Shakespeare festival in Stratford, Ontario for a little holiday. One afternoon, after months of spirited banter and innumerable challenges, we decided to play tennis. On her resume Janet was a hot shot player, Vassar varsity. I could hit the ball; I felt she'd probably kill me, but what the hell. I didn't mind the thought of being beaten in tennis by a pretty girl.

Janet got all dolled up in a really flattering white knit miniskirt ensemble with pink embroidery—she had great long legs—and we took to the court in back of the hotel. She stood sideways at the baseline and held the ball straight out at chest level before her, like a beginning student—elbow locked, hand down, the ball in her fingers.

Then she dropped the ball, let it bounce, bent her knees, took a *big* wind-up, and swiped underhand. The ball sailed over my head, over the fence.

And then Janet developed a terrible migraine. We went back to the room.

Back at Janet's apartment at the Ontario, dozens of reporters were camped on the grass outside. In these days before twenty-four hour cable news, the media was kinder and more gracious. Every day, the doorman would give Loretta Cooke a new stack of business cards left politely by journalists seeking an interview. The only reporter who made it past the front desk was *New York Times* powerhouse Maureen Dowd, though she didn't get an interview. Meanwhile, inside the apartment, Loretta Cooke taped garbage bags to the windows for privacy. Stratman set about untangling Janet's finances. He wrote checks for all her debts but refused to sign them until Janet took a pair of scissors to her credit cards. Janet was taking twenty milligrams of Valium every four hours. She complied with her father's request.

In time the reporters went away; Elsa Walsh moved out. Janet took a smaller apartment and began dating another resident of the Ontario, a Jewish lawyer from Toledo named Joe Phillips. They were married in Washington—big dress, big cake, big bill. Her father paid but refused to attend. After the wedding, Loretta Cooke filed for divorce. Joe's parents were present but did not seem happy with their son's decision to marry Janet.

Janet and Joe settled into a condo in the Maryland suburbs. At first she tried working on her memoirs. It was also reported that a publishing house had advanced her $50,000 to try her hand at fiction, but no contract was ever signed. She wrote a few stories for *Cosmopolitan*, but none ran. One story for *Washingtonian* about escort services began, "Call her Samantha. . . ."

After about a year, needing something to do, Janet went to work behind the jewelry counter at Bloomingdale's. When a news crew showed up, acting on a tip, she finished out the week and quit.

Janet and Joe had gone to France on their honeymoon, and once she was there, she knew for sure that this was the place she was meant to live. By coincidence a diplomatic job soon opened up. The couple moved to Paris in 1985, and it was wonderful, living there was just as she'd always imagined. They had a beautiful flat on the avenue du Président-Kennedy in the sixteenth arrondissement with a view of the Eiffel Tower.

Because France has always been a haven for expats and exiles, because the French have always had a special love for writers and writing, Janet found herself in a most agreeable atmosphere. The French, she says, tended to look upon her transgression as an *erreur de jeunesse,* a childish mistake. Everyone she met urged her to get back to her writing. "You must not lose your voice" is how they put it. In Paris, Janet was happier and had more fun and more friends than ever before in her life.

Less pleasing was her marriage, which became, in stages, unhappy, lonely and then stormy. After more than a decade, she petitioned for divorce. She did not fare well against an American attorney with diplomatic protection in a French court.

Finally, in 1994, after enduring an entire winter with no electricity in her apartment, Janet called home and asked her mom for a plane ticket.

Walking to the gate at Charles de Gaulle airport, she noticed a man following her with a camera. She stopped, turned, grabbed his long lens.

It turned out he was on assignment for *People* magazine's twenty-fifth anniversary issue, the "Where Are They Now?" feature.

"A pitiful tale, is it not?" says Janet, dissolving into her trademark laugh. She is sitting on the bench in the Crossroads mall, outside Hudson's department store, due shortly to begin her shift at Liz Claiborne.

Since her return from Europe, Janet says, "I've learned a lot of things about how most people really live. And lemme tell you, it ain't pretty."

In Toledo, Janet worked at the Limited Express for $4.85 an hour. With no car and cuts in local bus service, she was forced to walk miles home some nights hewing a path along the center line for safety. One frigid evening, icicles formed on her long eyelashes. For some reason, her mother—who was feeding, clothing, and housing her eldest with no apparent misgivings—would not let her borrow the car. Before she went in the hospital for surgery, Loretta Cooke bought a steering wheel lock and hid the key.

Hence Kalamazoo. Some friends, a job, anonymity, a quiet struggle.

These days, when Janet goes food shopping, she makes hard choices. Vegetables or chicken? Fish or potatoes? She might want Quaker Oats, but she settles for generic. She understands now why poor people are often fat. Starch is cheaper than protein or veggies.

During her childhood, Stratman was obsessed with the light bill; Janet keeps it dark to lower the bills. She's always loved candles. They were particularly nice when she first moved in and all she had in the living room was a beach chair. Janet can't afford to have drinks with the girls after work. Even if she has a few extra dollars, she has to weigh the mileage, the cost of gas. Dry cleaning is out. Her bathroom looks like a Chinese laundry. She has bad asthma but can't afford a doctor. Because her job isn't quite full-time, she doesn't receive health benefits. Certainly, she is a valued employee. Ever the overachiever, she was hesitant to take time off for interviews. Currently, she's two months behind on her car payments because of an illness in January. To cut costs, Janet has to keep the heat low, which is bad for her breathing. She has a terrible cough.

"Even if you excluded everything that might be remotely considered extravagant, you still—I mean, when you're poor, if one thing goes wrong, you're screwed. And something always goes wrong when you're poor.

"I understand now how people get angry. I understand the postal worker syndrome. I understand how a person can just check out for a moment and do something awful because there's a degree of hopelessness, there's a feeling like you're resigned to something, only way back in your mind somewhere, you're not resigned to it, so you are angry. To me, of course, I rather favor suicide over homicide. I don't need to go to jail. I feel like I've been in jail for half my life."

In the course of this story, Janet has been portrayed as an unhappy child, an alienated young woman, a talented reporter, an infamous liar, a compromised exile, a nearly destitute shop clerk. A woman who was damaged by a bitter parent, who was himself damaged by the ugly history of race relations in this country. A woman who learned deceit as a means of survival at an early age; who never had a clear view of her capabilities or her place in the world; who lived much of her life, perhaps, on the verge of a nervous breakdown. The startling beauty who sashayed into the acre-square newsroom that January day has been reduced, in stages, to a forty-one-year-old divorced department store worker sitting at the kitchen table with a bowl of cereal at her elbow, chewing her nails (real now—acrylic is too expensive), brow knitted over her checkbook, trying to decide whether to pay her rent or her car note this month.

It is not a pretty picture, but it's the un-embroidered truth.

Had Janet committed her indiscretion more recently, perhaps her life would be different. Back in '81, when the press staked out her apartment at the Ontario, there were no cameras in the bushes, no guerrilla assaults on the building. While under siege, Janet was able to come and go at will, using a back entrance. Nowadays that door would be covered.

But while the media have become more voracious over the years, they have also taken on new and different roles, one of which is Father Confessor. People today know well that the surest route back to grace is a massive public appeal. You transgress; you confess; you are forgiven.

Having been away from home for so long, Janet missed much of this change. She doesn't think this article will automatically redeem her. She doesn't know what will happen exactly, though she knows things can't get worse. What she is hoping most is that people will understand what happened. She wasn't trying to pull off a massive hoax that would bring her fame. She was desperate; she was damaged. She did what she knew how to do.

Now, at last, she has done something else, something she has learned in her later life, in the years since "Jimmy's World." She has told the truth. It is a beginning.

Update: 35 Years Later
# "The Fabulist Who Changed Journalism"

Janet Cooke entered the acre-square newsroom of *The Washington Post* wearing a red wool suit and a white silk shirt. It was her first day of work. She was two hours late. She'd gotten lost walking the three blocks from her hotel.

It was the third day of 1980, the beginning of a new chapter for this 25-year-old black woman whose upper-middle class parents had sent their daughters to the finest white prep schools but insisted upon living close to their roots in Toledo. As Cooke made her way down the long aisle through the desk pods of the Metro Section, heads turned. Editors and reporters noted the shortness of her pleated skirt, the apparent self-possession of her gait, the length of her acrylic fingernails. In this post-Watergate era of big stories, star reporters, and "creative tension," most members of the Metro staff were young and well-pedigreed, true believers in the power of the fourth estate, captained by history's own Bob Woodward, who was trying his hand for the first time as an assistant managing editor. Deep inside the Beltway, in the heart of the nation's political culture, the *Post*'s was a newsroom like all others—and like no other, a distinct creature of the city it covered, rife with intrigue and machination. The customary greeting among its 900 staffers, working just blocks from the White House: "What's the gossip?"

At the moment, clearly, it was Janet Cooke.

Six months earlier her résumé had crossed Ben Bradlee's desk. The legendary executive editor—known for his silver hair and salty language, his friendship with JFK, and his willingness to stand behind aggressive reporting—had taken up a red grease pencil and circled "Phi Beta Kappa," "Vassar," and

"Black Journalists Association." At a time when the newspaper business was just beginning a journey toward workplace diversity, here was a *twofer*, a highly talented black woman with an impressive résumé. Bradlee passed Cooke's information to Woodward, with the message that the young Toledo *Blade* reporter should be recruited before *The New York Times* or the networks scooped her up.

On September 28, 1980, nearly nine months and 52 bylines after her first day at the *Post*, "Jimmy's World" was published on the front page. Cooke's story, about an 8-year-old heroin addict, created an instant sensation—the 1980s equivalent of "going viral"—reprinted around the country and around the world. As DC Mayor Marion Barry and city health and police officials hustled to find the child and prosecute his guardian-tormentors, the *Post* stood fast behind its First Amendment right to protect its reporter from having to reveal the boy's whereabouts. For this, the paper was heavily criticized, especially by black residents in the then-majority African-American city. Where journalists saw a blockbuster story, with bright writing and a deep social impact, civilians saw a child in need, and activists saw a captivating example of the black man's burden. Jimmy was never found.

On April 13, 1981, Cooke was awarded a Pulitzer. She won after the well-intentioned Pulitzer committee, enthusiastic about both Cooke's story and the possibility of awarding the first Pulitzer in journalism ever to an African-American woman, juggled her entry from the local-news category to the feature-writing category in order to assure her a prize.

Proud of its former employee, the Toledo *Blade* quickly prepared a story. It went to press at 8am. Later that morning, according to an exhaustive investigation by *Post* ombudsman Bill Green, *Blade* editors read biographical sketches of the Pulitzer winners that moved over the Associated Press wire. The sketches were based on the résumés submitted with the entries. The *Blade*'s bio for Janet, taken from its own personnel records, differed considerably. On her Pulitzer résumé, according to *Post* accounts, Cooke claimed to have graduated magna cum laude from Vassar College and to have received a master's degree from the University of Toledo. From what the *Blade* knew, she'd attended Vassar only for her freshman year and received a Bachelor of Arts from the University of Toledo. *Blade* editors alerted the wire service.

Sometime after 3 in the afternoon, Bradlee and Managing Editor Howard Simons received simultaneous phone calls. An AP editor wanted Simons. The assistant to the president of Vassar wanted Bradlee. Both callers were asking about Janet's résumé.

"Take her to the woodshed," Bradlee ordered, according to Green.

For nearly 11 hours—in various offices and conference rooms at the *Post*, in the Capitol Hilton bar, and even in City Editor Milton Coleman's car as the two drove around Southeast DC looking for Jimmy's house—Janet was alternately interrogated, cajoled, comforted, pressured, and flattered by Bradlee, Woodward, Simons, Coleman, and others.

Finally, at 1:45 am, Cooke confessed to Woodward's Deputy AME David Maraniss. "There is no Jimmy and no family," she said, according to Maraniss. "It was a fabrication. I want to give the prize back."

Disgraced, the *Post* returned the Pulitzer. (The prize was re-awarded to Teresa Carpenter of *The Village Voice*.)

"The paper absolutely changed that moment," says Donald E. Graham, the *Post*'s publisher at the time, scion of the family that owned and ran the paper for eight decades, until its sale in 2013 to Amazon founder Jeff Bezos.

And from that moment forward, journalism changed, too. Cooke became infamous, the first in a line of publicly exposed fabulists including Stephen Glass of *The New Republic*, Jayson Blair of *The New York Times*, and Jack Kelley of *USA Today*.

Cooke's transgressions rocked the foundations of trust the press had built since the post-World War II blossoming of the information age. After centuries of Fleet Streeters, muckrakers, and yellow journalists, the public had welcomed Walter Cronkite into their living rooms; the crusading work of journalists had freed America from a bad war and a crooked presidency. All over the country, reporters were busy ferreting out corruption of all kinds. Now, suddenly, with Cooke, the press had fallen from grace.

Cooke's case also came to symbolize myriad other issues and transgressions in both journalism and the world at large, including the use of unnamed sources, minority recruitment, newsroom ethics, résumé fraud, and the tendency of some writers, operating in the genre known as creative nonfiction, to take license in the pursuit of more literary work.

"The Janet Cooke fabrication was shocking because it came at a time when most people respected newspapers and respected what we now call the media," says Howard Kurtz, a media critic and former Post staffer.

"Cooke was a warning shot," Kurtz says. "It was a harbinger of all kinds of journalistic scandals to come."

In the interest of disclosure, I know Janet Cooke.

The day she first appeared in the *Post* newsroom, I was 23, a former copy boy two years into a reporting job on the Metro staff.

Back then, the Metro staff was considered a training ground. In a newsroom stocked with legends like Bradlee and Woodward, we were known as "the kids," even though most of us were in our late 20s and 30s. I was a bit on the young side; most of the other staffers had been interns out of the Ivy Leagues or star writers at other papers before coming to

Metro. Also in the mix were a dozen or so women and minorities hired into two-year internships, a pipeline to newsroom diversity.

It was a heady time in the newspaper business, a golden age when the news budget was flush and the media carried a sheen of importance and invincibility. The *Post*'s own Woodward and Carl Bernstein had inspired a crowded field of young reporters to join the business in the interest of wearing the white hat of the public's right to know.

We were a tight-knit group, competitors and comrades both. We played co-ed touch football on Sundays on a field just north of the Washington Monument. (Even Woodward played on occasion. Maureen Dowd, then at *The Washington Star*, had nice speed and a good pair of hands.) We partied together at Woodward's Georgetown manse, at Maraniss's suburban house, at various bars all over town.

But most of all, we worked. Everyone had dark circles under their eyes, everyone was always rushing around, stumbling over themselves to find what our absolute leader, Woodward, liked to call a "Holy Shit" story. We wanted the brass ring—assignment to a special project that would showcase our talents and win an award; promotion to the National or Foreign or Style staff; a book or movie contract. Given our boss and role model, anything seemed possible.

At the same time, we were true believers in the standards set by Woodward and Bradlee. There was a star system, yes. There was creative tension, yes. But at the same time, we knew that shortcuts and screw ups or questionable information would not be tolerated. The idea of fabricating a quote, much less a character or an entire story, was unimaginable—akin to sinning in church.

Into this swirl came Janet Cooke, fresh from her hometown Toledo *Blade*. I met her late one night at her desk in the Weekly section, to which she'd been assigned. A zoned supplement to the paper, it was known as a training ground for affirmative-action hires and a dumping ground for older relics on their way to retirement. To the black members of the *Post* staff, the Weeklies were known as the Ghetto.

By the end of February, Cooke and I had begun dating. While we lasted officially only until June, our relationship continued in fits and starts for another year—a painful, exhilarating, 20-something psychodrama, during which time the Jimmy story was produced.

After the Pulitzer was returned, I was suspected of collaborating with Cooke on "Jimmy's World," my name having been found on the "edit trail" of the *Post*'s computer system. From the beginning, part of our relationship involved my services as an informal reader, not unusual among colleagues in any newsroom. Several times I made suggestions on "Jimmy's World" for style and flow; countless other times I read drafts for suggestions and support.

The truth is, I had my suspicions about the story from the beginning, but I couldn't bring myself to flat-out ask Janet if Jimmy was real. I'm not sure I wanted to know. To some extent, I suspected myself of being jealous—the piece had award-winner written all over it. In my favor was the fact that, months before the Pulitzer announcement, I voiced my concerns about the article to two older and respected reporters, Patrick Tyler and Joe Pichirallo, who formed one of Woodward's pet investigative teams. After the Pulitzer was returned, Woodward grilled me twice over two days. Had I something to confess, I surely would have.

In 1996, following Janet's return to the states after living in France for more than a decade, she decided to tell her story. She spoke to me at length for a piece published in *GQ*, entitled "Janet's World," the only substantial interview Cooke ever gave. The story details Cooke's difficult upbringing and her lifelong use of lies as a coping mechanism, primarily against the exceptionally high expectations and inflexible rules of her parents, her father particularly. It also documents her difficulties navigating the racial politics of the day—by some accounts, "Jimmy's World" would never have happened if not for the good intentions of those who thought their role was to level the playing field for minorities.

Thirty-five years since the Pulitzer was awarded and returned, interest in Cooke and her story—a cautionary tale at once so singular and so universal—has not waned.

Nearly every semester I get calls from reporters, producers, and journalism students seeking to track down Cooke for an interview. Most journalism schools offer some form of ethics course as part of their curriculum. I suspect all of them mention Cooke somewhere in the syllabus.

The influence of Cooke's transgressions runs through the corpus of modern journalism like blood through the circulatory system, leaving no area untouched. Racial and sexual diversity in the newsroom. The use of unnamed sources. The responsibility of editors to question reporters' stories—should all writers be considered guilty until proven accurate? The responsibility of writers to fact-check their own stories. The pressures of working on deadline and being judged by one's output. The perils of literary journalism. And the perils of human frailty—what responsibility does an institution have to look beyond a person's résumé and into his or her psyche?

"What caused Janet to do what she did was personal," says Walt Harrington, a former longtime *Post* staffer and editor and a colleague of Cooke's who went on to teach journalism at the University of Illinois. "As it happened, the organization pushed a flawed person into [something she couldn't handle]. It's like taking a person who's weak and encouraging them to do something that they're not equipped to resist. But at the same time, any system should be thoughtful about that kind of person."

I am nominally in touch with Cooke via email. I don't think I will betray her trust by reporting that she is living within the borders of the continental United States, within a family setting, and pursuing a career that does not primarily involve writing.

While I faithfully forward all requests for interviews, Cooke consistently declines to speak further of her role in the Pulitzer scandal. Clearly it has taken a toll.

"What more is there for anyone to write?" she said in response to my email about this story. And then she added, in her typical droll fashion, "Essentially, I've spent the last 30 years waiting to die."

Knowing her as I do, she was only half kidding.

Beyond Cooke's personal story—of an ambitious and talented but flawed young woman who dreamed of covering the White House—is the larger one, the unintended effect of her transgressions. Not only did she fabricate; she won the Pulitzer. Not only did she lie; she did so in the grandest fashion, on the biggest stage, and in the process disgraced her employers, pulling the wool over some of the brightest eyes in the business.

And if someone could do that right under the noses of Bradlee and Woodward and company, how could any reporter ever be trusted again?

Beautifully written and well-researched, "Jimmy's World" was a perfect storm of a story—a compelling combination of writer and subject matter and the politics of the day. It described an 8-year-old on heroin and the drug trade around him. The story ran about 2,100 words, starting on the front page, a little long for a standard newspaper feature but short compared to investigative projects that were in vogue. The article included Cooke's reporting about the city's burgeoning heroin trade, the emergence of the Golden Crescent in Asia as a major producer, and the impact of drugs on the community, years before the crack epidemic made this a common theme.

At the heart of the piece was a fourth-grader who lived in a heroin "shooting gallery" with his mother and her boyfriend, a drug dealer named Ron. "And every day, Ron or someone else fires up Jimmy, plunging a needle into his bony arm, sending the fourth-grader into a hypnotic nod," Cooke wrote.

The piece comes to a chilling end with Jimmy receiving his heroin fix as the reporter watches. "The needle slides into the boy's soft skin like a straw pushed into the center of a freshly baked cake.... 'Pretty soon, man,' Ron says, 'you got to learn how to do this for yourself.'"

For the *Post*, the Cooke debacle "was a tremendous jolt to the whole place," says former publisher Graham. "We, the *Post* collectively, didn't at first know how to respond. It seemed to me at the time that the best answer was first and foremost changing the way we hired people so that we were much more careful about reviewing what they said in their résumé."

For the late Ben Bradlee, says his biographer, Jeff Himmelman, "there was some real anguish about it. He felt like he had let the Grahams down, who had shown so much faith in him through Watergate. It was their paper and he didn't catch this, and he knew he didn't catch it, and there were a lot of other people who should have caught it, too, but it was his name at the top.... By far this was the big black eye of his career."

In a larger way, Graham says delicately, after the Cooke affair, something very fundamental began to shift in the *Post*'s and other newsrooms. Previously, there was "a tendency to trust your reporters," Graham says.

The audacity of Cooke's fabrication broke this bond of trust, both with editors and with readers. Suddenly, the institution known for bringing down liars and shining light on injustice was itself revealed to be a transgressor against the truth. As a reporter at the time, at the *Post* or anywhere else, you could feel the door slam. Before Cooke, we journalists wore the capes of crusaders who could do no wrong.

Today we face a different public perception. The line from Watergate, in 1972, to Cooke in 1980, to the vehicular death of the UK's Princess Diana in 1997—for which journalists were blamed—stretches a mere 25 years. Today, in the minds of many, the word "journalist" connotes invasive tabloid headlines and paparazzi.

Probably the biggest change wrought by the Cooke affair was the way reporters were allowed to use and manage unnamed sources. Prior to Cooke, reporters were trusted, the way Woodward was with Deep Throat—nobody asked for his identity. In the months following the Cooke affair, however, that practice began to change, recalls Jim Romenesko, a long-time observer of journalism. In the years to come, Romenesko posted on his site a number of memos from newspapers, including *USA Today*, declaring a new policy in which reporters were required to share the identities of unnamed sources with an editor. This practice remains an industry standard.

In a larger sense, there was a fundamental change in newsrooms. Before Cooke, newsrooms were more like the movies, peopled by a collection of committed, rogue oddballs. Since then, journalism has become more homogenized and standardized, more corporate, more rule-driven, though this has been due in part to economics. In sum: After Cooke, it was still cool to be a reporter, but it was also a little tainted. One of us had flown too close to the sun. All had been burned.

Harrington also points out that after Cooke, newspapers worked harder to be open with readers. For investigative series, literary recreations, or controversial stories, more column inches were devoted to source citations and explanatory editors' notes.

Another result, says Romenesko, was the rise of the era of the ombudsman at newspapers. The *Post*'s own Bill Green, with his evenhanded account of the *Post*'s failings in the Cooke affair, helped spark the trend. With the dual missions of advocating for the community of readers and functioning as a newspaper's internal moral compass, ombudsmen served to ease the trust issues that the Cooke affair literally and symbolically raised with the public. Even without ombudsmen, newspapers today put an ever greater emphasis on community relations, some of which can be traced to the post-Cooke efforts to quell community outrage.

For African-American journalists, say some, there was yet another layer of damage done. In a way, elements of Cooke's story are similar to the stories of many others. There is no better way to say it: Efforts at leveling the playing field are appreciated by those served. But the navigation is both tricky and somewhat embarrassing for the beneficiaries, many of whom are highly accomplished—if not, they wouldn't have come to anyone's attention in the first place.

"For all the glamor and prestige that Janet supposedly brought in with her to the *Post*, they put her straight into the Ghetto," says Courtland Milloy, a columnist for the *Post* and the only pre-Cooke-era staffer still working at the paper. "With all her credentials, Janet still went straight to the Weekly. That was just very telling to me."

"What happened with Cooke was a disappointment to African-American journalists," says Julianne Malveaux, a political commentator and past president of Bennett College, a historically black liberal arts college for women. "It was a hit. We all took it on the chin.

"People were excited when she got a Pulitzer and then [when it was returned], people were like, someone had pulled a rug out from under you," Malveaux says. "It basically eroded the integrity of a cadre of African-American journalists who do street reporting. It made people look at people of color, and African-Americans in particular, with more scrutiny. Janet Cooke gave white folks permission to be skeptical about black people in the newsroom."

Malveaux notes the perception that "anytime an African-American screws up, especially in the area of integrity, it essentially slimes all African-Americans. When a white guy screws up, like Stephen Glass, it doesn't slime on white people. They just say, okay, he was a jerk, and people move on."

For this reason, Malveaux says, she tries to remember that there was a troubled black woman at the center of the storm.

"In the end, I'm still concerned for Cooke. She made a major journalistic mistake, but she's a human being and deserves to be seen through that prism. She had great writing chops but she used them the wrong way."

Regardless of Cooke's personal story or actual intentions, her transgressions signaled the beginning of a radical change in the role of the media in American life. We live now in an age when no one fully trusts the media.

"One reason we're even still talking about what happened in 1981," Kurtz says, "is because Janet Cooke was to the news business what Vietnam and Watergate were to political establishments."

Cooke returning the Pulitzer, he adds, "was the moment that public trust gave way to cynicism....Each subsequent episode tarnishes us all."

# PERMISSIONS

Parts of *Janet's World* were first published in *GQ* in June, 1996, and also in *Scary Monsters and Super Freaks*, first published by Thunder's Mouth Press in 2003, republished by Dacapo Press in 2007. Reprinted with permission of the author.

"The Fabulist Who Changed Journalism," first published by the *Columbia Journalism Review*, Spring 2016. Reprinted with permission of the author.

# ALSO BY MIKE SAGER

*The Lonely Hedonist*

*Stoned Again*

*The Devil and John Holmes*

*High Tolerance, A Novel*

*The Someone You're Not*

*Revenge of the Donut Boys*

*Scary Monsters and Super Freaks*

*Vetville: True Stories of the U.S. Marines*

*Hunting Marlon Brando*

# ABOUT THE AUTHOR

Mike Sager is a bestselling author and award-winning reporter. For more than forty years he has worked primarily as a writer for the *Washington Post, Rolling Stone, GQ* and *Esquire*. Sager is the author or editor of more than a dozen books, including anthologies, novels, a biography, eBooks, and textbooks. In 2010 he won the National Magazine Award for profile writing. Several of his stories have inspired films and documentaries; he is editor and publisher of The Sager Group LLC. For more information, please see www.MikeSager.com.

# MORE FROM THE SAGER GROUP

*The Stories We Tell: Classic True Tales by America's Greatest Women Journalists*

*Newswomen: Twenty-five Years of Front-Page Journalism*

*New Stories We Tell: True Tales by America's New Generation of Great Women Journalists*

# ABOUT THE PUBLISHERS

NeoText is a publisher of quality fiction and long-form journalism. Visit the NeoText website at NeoTextCorp.com.

The Sager Group was founded in 1984. In 2012 it was chartered as a multimedia content brand, with the intent of empowering those who create art—an umbrella beneath which makers can pursue, and profit from, their craft directly, without gatekeepers. TSG publishes books; ministers to artists and provides modest grants; and produces documentary, feature, and commercial films. By harnessing the means of production, The Sager Group helps artists help themselves. For more information, please see TheSagerGroup.net.

www.ingramcontent.com/pod-product-compliance
Lightning Source LLC
Chambersburg PA
CBHW030346100526
44592CB00010B/845